AF237005

2

Dr. Lutz Knoche

Traumata of Mankind
Part One
Global coming out

The book has been revised from the German original "Human Traumata Teil I" and translated into English by Gauss

This book is a new version of the book "EROS- 300,000 years of evolutionary history"

Manufacture and publishing
BoD Books on Demand, Norderstedt
ISDN 9783753442785

To the author

Dr. Lutz Knoche worked for many years as a psychotherapist and coach. In the last few years, he has started to write guides based on his knowledge and practical experience. In his books, he includes case studies from his practice and presents tried and tested exercises for immediate help. In addition to classical psychology, he has developed therapeutic hypnosis and bioenergetic methods and applied them successfully. He worked with many people from all walks of life, with socially disadvantaged young people, couples, young entrepreneurs in success coaching, politicians, entrepreneurs, managers, and artists. Now he mainly wants to make his knowledge and experience accessible to many people through publications.

5

Human trauma
Part One
Global coming out

Contents

1. Prolog

It is written in the great religions of the world. Adam and Eve once lived in Paradise. One day the serpent whispered in Eve's ear to pluck the forbidden fruit from the tree of knowledge and eat it with Adam. Finally, she did and handed the apple of that tree to Adam. They both ate it. Now Adam recognized the nakedness of his companion and a shiver went through him, which seized his whole senses. Carefully and curiously, he caressed Eva's breast and saw how her nipples became very hard. Eva's body trembled with excitement. She had never seen anything like it. Then she saw the restless eyes of her companion and looked at him too in his nakedness. She saw that his member which he carried between his legs was getting bigger and stiffer. She also took her hand and carefully stroked this rearing part. As soon as she touched it, it twitched powerfully in her hands and Adam groaned softly. But it was a happy moan. Like she had never heard from him before. That excited her even more and she also felt a tingling sensation between her legs. Adam also took his hand and led her there. He noticed her labia swell and it got wet between them. He ran his fingers carefully through the gap that opened wider. Always up and down. Eva senses that there must be a big, sweet secret hidden inside her. Adam also noticed the increasing excitement of Eve, which he evoked with his fingers. That spurred him on to go deeper and faster. Eve did the same to Adam's now hard, excitedly pumping member. She now clutched that with her hand. Both moaned in their unprecedented excitement. And didn't know what was happening to them. But it was wonderful. Eva spread her legs so that Adam could slide deeper and deeper through her now very wet column. She felt more and more how wonderful this secret must be. Her body swayed. She lay on her back and pulled Adam towards her. All by itself, he slipped his stiff member into the vagina of his companion. As if out of their minds, they moaned and moved their bodies in wild ecstasy. They drove it until evening because they could not find an end. But then God came and saw what they were doing. For a while, he watched them secretly, full of interest, but then heard Eve calling out: "Oh my God, that's beautiful." But Adam replied: "Why God, it is me who gives you this happiness." When God heard, he realized that people no longer need him to be blissful. The Tree of Knowledge had shown them that there was much better than being in paradise. They didn't need a god for that. Then he went wild with anger and drove her out of paradise. Since then, the self-appointed representatives of God on earth have been preaching that sex is sin and immoral. It is only allowed in secret and under strict observance of the rules. And fears were stoked. And even today, most people still have a disturbed relationship with it.

When the story of Adam and Eve was written, the world was already very different. Humans had lived on earth for hundreds of thousands of years and entertained them with joy, polygamous and bisexual with one another. Just as it has happened in nature for millions of years. If you want to understand this book, overcome your shyness. Now call out loudly and with joy three times: SEX, SEX, SEX! Lose your scruples because you have been lied to. Sex is not embarrassing at all, and it is certainly not a sin. Yes, it is true, you were lied to and betrayed for 2000 years, thereby robbing you of a lot of joy in life. The monogamous, heterosexual marriage, preached by the church, in which the woman was subordinated to the man, and the two millennia-long prohibitions of love in all its diversity, is a crime against humanity. This led to a lot of suffering and alienation of our natural evolutionary development. Most societies have not yet freed themselves of this. I'll show you that in this book. It was the greatest brainwashing that has ever come upon mankind. The church has given false testimony about sexuality. Over time, people believed that, and many still do today. These rules were and are unnatural. It has led us into a collective trauma to this day. A trauma is full of fears and moral misconceptions. This book will get you out of there. It's a coming out of this straitjacket we're in.

Homo sapiens began to reflect on his world about 300,000 years ago. He realized that he could live out the sexual pleasure for his pleasure whenever he wanted and with whomever he wanted. The first people did that wildly and unrestrainedly. Similar behaviors existed before them, and they still exist in all animal species today. What the sex life of animals looks like has been kept secret for a long time. The facts turn our still prevailing conception of normal and abnormal, of natural and unnatural, completely upside down. Here are the facts. Here is an excerpt from GEO online magazine:

"Science now assumes that animals have sex because it is fun and pleasurable for them - and not, as naturalist Charles Darwin put it, just to preserve the species. Monkeys of both sexes have even been shown to have an orgasm.

The brain waves and muscle contractions were measured in the animals.

A same-sex relationship is preferred.

The range of erotic relationships and same-sex activities in the animal kingdom is large: female dolphins, for example, slide their fins into the partner's genital area. Whales rub against each other with erect penises, male manatees process the sex of their partner for lack of hands with their fins, dwarf chimpanzee males suck on the penis of another male and river dolphins stick their penis into their conspecifics blowhole...

Some species even resolve their conflicts or leadership issues with same-sex sex - such as male lions. They have sex with the competitor to ensure mutual loyalty and to lead the pack amicably.

"Www.geo.de/natur/tierwelt/13372-rtkl-homosexualitaet-im-tierreich

Behavioral biology - gays, lesbians, and bisexuals - quite normal in the animal kingdom

Whether fish, birds, or mammals - as studies show, around 1500 animal species practice same-sex pairing...

There are many reasons animals engage in same-sex activities. Sometimes because no partner of the opposite sex is available at the moment. At other times, they just enjoy it, socialize or settle disputes.

In the animal kingdom, there is simply no homophobia, if only heterophobia. Most of the animals are not homosexual, but rather bisexual. They also mate with the opposite sex, for example to father offspring.

www.dw.com/de/schwule-lesben-und-bisexuelle-im-tierreich-ganz-normal/a-39966868

Another scientific contribution

Ancestors of all modern animals were bisexual

So far, scientists assumed that heterosexuality dominated the animal kingdom. But they were wrong! The latest research from the university also suggests that homosexuality is much more widespread in the animal kingdom than previously thought. And: It could have been part of animal behavior from the start ... because it has always been there". They even go a step further and state that heterosexual behavior is believed to be an "inferred trait" that evolved from the bisexual nature of the ancestral species along with homosexual behavior.

www.bild.de/lgbt/2019/lgbt/studie-soll-beweisen-homo-und-bisexualitaet-ist-die-norm-im-tierreich-66130656.

From that point of view, God was very clever. He knew from the animal kingdom of the dominant bisexuality. That is why he created Adam and Eve. If he had created Adam and Peter or Eve and Heidi, the fall would probably have come much earlier. You don't need a lot of imagination to be able to imagine how two naked young girls or two naked boys who are alone in paradise can easily and openly discover their lust together. God wanted to avoid that. But in the end, he didn't succeed, despite the unequal couple chosen.

So what is unnatural? Let us pause for a moment and realize: Bisexuality is the proven natural form of all living beings. Homo- and heterosexuality have emerged from this and form a minority. Sexual practices, whatever, are not directed against nature or are unnatural. That means we were lied to. A large part of us is not interpreted exclusively as heterosexual and monogamous. And that corresponds to our nature, which opens the way for us to enjoy life and social cohesion.

It is therefore not surprising that the overwhelming majority of behavioral biologists had long known about these sexual practices in the animal world. They just didn't report about it. So great is still the fear of speaking openly about sex in our day and age. Especially since many prevailing beliefs are questioned here and a completely new awareness about sex opens up. If we can assume today that the sexual experiences in the animal kingdom were and are dominantly bisexual, this also applies to humans. Arguments like: Man is not an animal and "civilized" and therefore has a different sex relationship is absurd. Why should he change sexual behavior when bisexuality has naturally emerged as the most suitable form in development? So we humans have been very diverse in our lust from the start. The conscious shaping of our sexuality had the consequence that we were generally polygamous and bisexual and still are in our dispositions. It was precisely this sexual development that made us who we are today. It strengthened our social connections and the love for one another, which was and is necessary for our further development. The stronger social ties germinated the feeling of love, which through our conscious recognition of the world in which we live, became a universal force in the development of human beings. That made people unique.

We have only turned away from this normality in the past two thousand years. And we owe that originally to the Catholic teachings that still spread these absurd teachings about unnatural sex today. The enormous social and spiritual destructive impact on people in these two thousand years through heresy is incomprehensible. This is probably why millions of people died during this time. The overwhelming majority of people have not yet freed themselves from this demon. On the contrary, there are still millions of people who fanatically allow themselves to be blinded by this nonsense. You continue to defend falsehood. These doctrines of the Church are unnatural and despicable. They are so abnormal that even church officials cannot adhere to them. The sexual revolution and the social revolution that is inseparable from it are still in their infancy today.

Every development has a meaning in evolution and should lead to higher development, even if this does not always happen harmoniously and without complications. The free sexual development of man was thus an important milestone in his higher development. Humans have been able to develop further for hundreds of thousands of years, borne by the mutual pleasure of each other. In his social behavior, there was therefore no difference between man and woman during this long period of human development. Everyone had his or her place in society on an equal footing. There was absolutely no reason why it shouldn't be. Even if there were occasional disruptions in this development in some regions, this social equality of the sexes, in its complementary diversity, made us the people we are today.

That changed after the end of the peaceful era of the arable farmers and cattle breeders due to the violent conquests. This made the land the property of a few. The man waged wars and became the owner. He dominated society and women were dispossessed and dependent on him. This heralded the temporary demise of the long-standing gender equality. This gradually changed the relationship between men and women fundamentally. The fulfillment of sexual pleasure became more and more a pleasure satisfaction and moved closer to the animal kingdom. The important social significance of an equal, mutually supportive further development between the sexes became less important. Social life was determined by established rules of the ruling class of men and, if necessary, enforced by force. Sex became either a duty or a commodity. With the emergence of private property, social conditions changed and people stopped developing socially and sexually. The consequences of this can still be felt today.

This negative development reached its climax with the arrival of the Catholic Church about 2000 years ago, which later served the ruling class as a perfect instrument of power. Now the woman was officially the man's subject, and over time sex was forbidden in almost all relationships - except in straight marriage. And at that time this could only be legitimized by the church. The man was forcefully forced into monogamy and heterosexuality. He could only do that if the church had given its blessing beforehand. Humanity was thus humiliated and oppressed. Since then, to this day, we have been in constant sexual imbalance for the most part. This made us dissatisfied and developed arguments, envy, jealousy, violence, child abuse, and much more. Our world would look much better today if it had not been for this criminal influence on our free sexual development by the Church.

Nevertheless, two thousand years is a short time in the human development period and these unnatural and grotesque rules and norms of these religions have also been questioned again and again. Today many people see it differently and society is also creating more and more freedom for sexual self-determination. But we are still a long way from a natural, free fulfillment of lust. The wrong rules and norms that have been shaped for thousands of years are still too tight in many minds. Even the laws and "moral" norms in our society are still shaped by these influences. They influence us from our birth. Prejudices and beliefs are already created in childhood and firmly anchored in us, without us being able to consciously influence them at this age. Later on, many are firmly convinced of these moral principles, even if they are wrong and reduce their quality of life. This leads to increasing problems in our day and age. Even in our epoch, the overwhelming part of people does not live out their natural, wonderful free lust and we are currently still further away from the social support provided by free sexuality. But the conditions to find our way again are in place. More than ever before. If it is still a rocky road to get there, we can start today and become happier again. In this book, I present approaches and suggestions.

To understand our sexual desires and to be able to live them out freely and happily, it is necessary to examine the natural development of human sexuality. This helps us understand our problems today. Through prejudices and wrong beliefs, the history of sexual development is often described from a morality derived from it. Sometimes misinterpreted or withheld facts. Much is simply not mentioned, dismissed as atypical, or put in a completely wrong context. So we are still being misled. Sometimes this is done consciously, but for the most part, because the people who deal with it are of course also subject to their prejudices and the beliefs of our time. This will displace historical finds. This is nothing new with many kinds of representations of historical processes. It is often based on one's own beliefs and prejudices. And there are certainly many more unbiased reports on this that are in the secret archives of the Catholic Church and are not accessible to us.

We have to radically change the view of history about ourselves because there are too many truths that have been hushed up so far. I invite you on an exciting journey through 300,000 years of human sexual development. I want to garnish this historical development with fictional stories from the individual epochs that could have happened if one follows some prehistoric and historical findings. But my aim is not to write a new history of humanity, because I am not a historian. I want to show you some of what we lost 2000 years ago in an entertaining way so that we can finally find it again. It is intended to open up a new way of looking at sexual freedom that has never been presented before and to lead them to find themselves. For some, this can be shocking at times, too. But our sexual development did not start 2,000 years ago, but a million years ago. Many modern so-called moral norms in today's human community contradict our nature, which is evolutionary in us and has a deep meaning for our happy further development. Therefore, it is important to write honestly about it, even if some are upset about it at first. I believe that ultimately it is important for us to survive that sex finally regains the status it deserves.

It is our wonderful nature, even if it has long been suppressed. Everyone can feel and recognize this when they free themselves from the blockages that have been drummed into them. We can change it again and live more freely than ever before.

2. The path from the reproductive instinct to conscious experience

According to current knowledge, the representatives of the genus Homo developed from a species of Australopithecus two to three million years ago. It was here that fossil tool finds were discovered for the first time. This leads to the conclusion that he was consciously changing the environment to his advantage. He began to recognize the world, reflect on it, and developed self-confidence. In this way, he gradually became aware of his sexual pleasure, which he no longer wanted to satisfy exclusively for procreation, but wanted to live it out in ever more diverse ways. In the animal kingdom, there were already numerous role models for this, but he now applied them even more purposefully and more frequently.

At this time, evolution also created physical and biological characteristics of human sexuality, including hidden ovulation.
The fertility of female animals is usually communicated through physical or behavioral signals so that fertilization can take place during this phase. In homosexuals, ovulation was "hidden". The consequence of this was that the sexual act was less strongly linked to procreation. The consciously controlled sexual behavior of the homo went beyond the genetic exchange. The strongest, the instinct of the homo species was given an increasingly important social function. This resulted in a multitude of sexual, polygamous orientations. It was a natural process of development.
According to previous knowledge, Homo sapiens, which developed 300,000 years ago, did not have a firm connection to a specific person at that time. It is often portrayed this way in public, but it comes exclusively from

the ideas of the authors of such stories. Of course, there is no evidence of monogamous relationships from this period. That would also be very unlikely.

The sex ratio in the clans, some of which had their camp far away from each other, was not always balanced. And because of the division of labor between men and women, they were often separated from one another for a long time. It is logically understandable that they followed their feelings of pleasure and developed and led a bisexual way of life. That applied to both men and women. Even before and even today there is same-sex satisfaction in the entire animal kingdom. It was therefore nothing new to her from the start. But through the conscious living out of their sexual urges, which could now be lived out at any time and opportunity, and the development to a self-confident social being, it became a dominant form. This also strengthened their social ties.

Another important indication of this is that evolution adapted the body to the new sexual behavior. And again she created the prerequisites to promote this diverse development by evoking greater physical pleasure even in the same-sex act. It was an enrichment for people and drove development forward. After thousands of years of this evolutionary process and the indulgence of sexual pleasure with both sexes, all the physical prerequisites for this had developed.

The men now not only had exciting feelings on their penis, but also a pleasurable G-spot inside on the prostate, and the women had their clitoris directly on their vagina and not further inside, where they could only have experienced these feelings with men. The most natural and plausible explanation for this physical development is the general bisexual way of life. As a result, people could have fun with each other more pleasurably and at any time. Evolution had created better conditions for man in the sense of a higher development of sexuality.

It led to an even stronger social bond between both sexes and one another, which ensured the survival and further development of humanity. The diverse orientation and the bisexual, polygamous, socially bound way of life in the community were the reasons why we prevailed over other genres. It can be seen as the genetic code of the sexual evolutionary development of humans, which made us who we are today.

2.1. The free fulfillment of lust in the clan

A small group of Homo sapiens had set up camp on the edge of the forest. It consisted of 6 women, 8 men, and 12 children. Your place was well chosen. A large, steep rock wall loomed behind him to protect them from attackers or wild animals. Next to their camp, there was a stream of clear water that flowed into a small lake. It was only 100 meters from them.

The first thing they did was build a fireplace. It was the main place of work for food production and social life. Then they built a big hut in which they all lived and slept together, and in the end, they protected their camp from wild animals with a high fence. Everyone lends a hand. The women were built even stronger back then. Due to their varied work in the clan, they had more physically difficult tasks to do. As a result, the differences between men and women in their physique were not so clearly pronounced.

After five days they finished building their camp and in the evening sat happily by the campfire. After a while, Ako the clan leader began to hug and caress the woman sitting next to him. His sexual desires were kindled and he proudly presented his excited member. When the woman saw that she was also quite aroused. So right at the campfire they gave free rein to their lust and united with each other. That excited the others who saw it and they couldn't hold back either. So they all made love by the fire that evening.

Two men were left without a wife. A young man named Ira, who primarily shared his lust with men, and another boy who had only recently reached sexual maturity, but was already dedicated to the satisfaction of clan members in all possible ways. It was also a pleasure for both of them to have fun together. A little later Ako came to Ira. It had separated from its female partner and now also reunited with this wild young man and let him ride it long and passionately. Since they had not had time for such amusements in the last few days due to their work in setting up their camp, it turned into a long night of ecstatic encounters. At first, the children watched curiously but then fell asleep by the fire.

Only one boy stayed awake and had an erection while watching. When a woman saw this, she called him over. Everyone left each other and looked at him and his stiff member because for the group it was always a special event when a boy became sexually mature. Would they get a new male member that night? He was nine years old. When he was with the woman, she took his stiff penis in her hand and rubbed it slowly. It wasn't long before seed came out of him for the first time. He screamed as he did so. The audience was very impressed. Everyone congratulated him and was happy about it. Ako told him: "You became a man today. You can experience this happiness full of joy from now on. Use it as often as you can. "

From that day on they had one more man in their clan. He was trained by the men so that he could accompany them on the hunt next time. On the first night of his new life, he learned how to make a woman happy. What two women liked to teach him? The boy had gotten a taste for it and, after completing his training with the men, ran to the women every evening. And after he had let off steam for a while, Ira showed him the varieties of men, which also gave him great pleasure. And since he was young and wanted to experience these exciting new feelings unchecked and unrestrained, he was gladly welcome by everyone. Not infrequently, after he was with the women, he ran to the men to then savor the other side of his lust. From this time on he had a happy and joyful life in the clan.

22

Ako had chosen the place well. A strong and skilled hunter himself, he was 25 years old. Back then in middle age. In his clan, they all lived together in a hut-like a big family. He did not know how many children he had of the twelve that were born. There weren't very strong ties between women and men.

Although he had a favorite, he was often with someone else. Just like they all did. Ako was not only a good hunter but also a potent lover and loved by both sexes for it.

That day he decided to go hunting with the men to get meat for the camp. Since the women were also good fighters to defend themselves in the event of an attack on the camp, all eight men went on the hunt with Ako. So it was good that they could give each other amusement because nobody knew how long it would take them to successfully kill an animal. Her sexual urges and desires were simply too strong to forego gratification for a long time. Why should they? The hunt lasted five days before they shot a deer. During this time they enjoyed themselves by the fire every evening and enjoyed in ecstatic pleasure massaging their pleasure points with each other with their limbs. So they fell asleep satisfied and happy.

From the Celts, there is the oldest, secured, and written tradition on bisexuality. Here is an excerpt from Wikipedia:

"The second testimony goes back to Poseidonios, who wrote very extensively and reliably about the customs of the Celts. His work has not survived, but there are many quotations from later authors, such as Diodor Siculus (1st century BC):

"… Rather, they are seized with a wild passion for hugs with men. They usually lie on the floor on animal skins and roll around with a sleeper on either side. But the most unbelievable thing is: They are not concerned about their

decency, but willingly surrender the flower of their bodies to others; and they do not consider it shameful, but rather consider it dishonorable if one of them is courted and does not accept the favor offered. "
- Diodor Siculus: Historical Library 5.32.7 [2] "

I think anyone who describes the men's anus as the "flower of their body" has also had very nice experiences with it. It is doubtful whether the phrase, "They are not concerned about their decency", has been translated correctly. As is so often the case, the wrong translations were probably chosen here, which corresponded to the translator's views. It is not about something extraordinary, but something completely natural, to have fun anally among men, which is evident from the text. The Celts were a highly developed people, with a rich culture and mysticism that many people still find fascinating today. They were also known as fearless and strong warriors. Grave goods showed that women could also play a high social role. They enjoyed their bisexual way of life, full of pleasure, and thus strengthened their social bond with each other, which contributed to high culture and social strength.

Ako and his men were looking forward to their wives after they had been on the road for several days, but they also followed their joyful and lustful amusement with one another. An exception was da Ira, the young hunter from their group. He preferred to play with the men. Which the others liked very much. Ako, along with his favorite girl in the camp, particularly liked the pleasure of being with him. An individual attractiveness towards other clan members had already developed in him. But the exercise of pleasure was stronger. So he also enjoyed himself with whoever offered himself when he felt like it. In this way, he promoted their cohesion. The intense social connections gave birth to a deeper feeling for one another, which was not geared towards a specific person. It was the tender unfolding of love.

But not only the men but also the women had fun with each other in the camp. They rubbed their bodies so that they reached their clit. Rubbed it with her fingers and played with her nipples. They also promoted their coexistence at the same time.

When the men had killed enough game on the hunt, they returned to the camp, where a big party was held that evening and they were together again in ecstatic pleasure. Having found a good place for their camp, they decided to stay for a long time. While the men were out hunting, the women discovered a cave in the rock face. From then on they slept there and found better protection there in the event of a storm and from wild animals. There were water, game, and plants and they lived contentedly in this place. With the addition of men, they were now 9 men and six women.

One day two strangers came to their camp with a wild boar that had been killed. They offered this to the group as a gift. So they were welcomed and curiously eyed. They came from the north and had clothes on. When she asked Ako about it, they explained that it was colder in the north and that they had to put on clothes. He replied that they were here now and that they no longer needed it. The strangers noticed that the group was uncomfortable. So they put them off.

They weren't used to being naked and got an erection with that nakedness. Since they had brought such a valuable gift with them, Ako offered him to have fun with a woman or a man of his clan so that they could relax again. They accepted that with thanks. Young Ira was also chosen by one of the guests and a woman by the other.

25

The men from the north spent many months in the cold. Pleasurable games, naked by the fire, were not possible there. As a result of this restriction, they looked for new ways of being able to be with each other with pleasure and discovered oral sex for themselves. They didn't have to be naked and could still experience orgasmic feelings with each other at any time. It was something completely new for Ira and the young woman of the clan when the strangers had fun with them in this way, but it was very exciting. And the others watched in amazement and learned in the process. They quickly tried each other while the two strangers continued to follow their lust. From this time on it was even more exciting for them and they could live out their strong urges faster and more often. It was the first satisfaction that did not come through a union and was enjoyed by men and women alike. With this, the pleasurable togetherness moved further and further away from the actual reproduction. Yes, even the children playfully included it in their children's games. They saw it with the adults every evening.

After the two men had ended their happy being together, they presented their concerns to the clan. They reported that they had had a long and arduous journey. Some of their group died in the process. That left only two men, four women, and three children. That would be too little to survive. That is why they would like to join Ako. Since Ako had previously admired their new weapons for hunting, which were better than his, and he knew that mixing the clans would be beneficial for the offspring, he wanted to take them up. But not before they met everyone else and everyone agreed. Because he didn't want any trouble in his group. So they brought the four women and the children to them, and when they had got to know each other enjoyably in the evening around the campfire, they were welcomed. It was a win for everyone. The clan lived contentedly and happily for many generations. Over time, other groups came and settled nearby. Some banded together. So Ako got further growth and his group got bigger and bigger. Others brought new knowledge with them. This developed the knowledge of the tribe, but also their worldview. People became aware of their mortality and began to worry about it. Death could not be accepted like this and they believed in living on in another world. They worshiped more and more gods and communicated with their deceased ancestors. Their awareness of the world in which they lived also expanded. Certainly, this sometimes changed their sexual behavior, and the first rites for it arose. Even today, in some primitive peoples, men still meet and take each other's semen orally. They like to consume it as the strongest vital energy juice. It means strength and long life.

2.2. New social orientations through the emergence of large families

The tribe grew and its members could no longer do everything together because it made no sense if 30 men went hunting together.

The human race multiplied and the living space became narrower. This was particularly the case in areas where living conditions were good. Because of this, the peace was constantly endangered by other tribes in the vicinity, so that some men had to stay in the camp for defense. The women were now more preoccupied with the many children and the food. Very few had time to learn how to use the increasingly complex weapons.

The craft developed through the transfer of knowledge. So better weapons were made, utensils for the household, but also works of art such as jewelry. There was a division of labor within the tribe. This led to a gradual specialization and thus to the individualization of the tribal members. Talents and talents could develop and so people differed more and more in their appearance and behavior. The intelligence and the acquisition of knowledge of the individual could develop better, which he then passed on to the others. As a result, people became more and more self-conscious and developed a stronger self-confidence. This affected their sexual behavior. Individual sexual desires arose. The choice of partner became more and more targeted, depending on the type.

Now more than 100 people no longer wanted to live in one big house, but many smaller houses were built in which they lived in large families. However, there was the community house of the village for the day, where everything took place in the community. So they cooked and ate together and the children grew up together. Since the men, due to their strength and strength, were responsible for the security and the hunt, the most important source of food until then, they became the head of an extended family. So they found one or more women and founded this new community with them within the tribe.

The women had an equal position in the group through the children, the food preparation, and the gathering of plants. There was no difference in the social status in the clan between men and women. Nevertheless, for the first time, something like a selection of the sexes took place in the tribe. The women were keen to find a strong and smart man who could father healthy children in the extended family and make sure that they grew up well-nourished. The men were keen to have one or more fertile and healthy women who could bear them strong children, breastfeed adequately, and do their chores around the house.

Therefore, people's physical attributes became more and more important. They began to take care of their bodies, adorn themselves, and courted the opposite sex. The relationship between man and woman gradually changed completely. The physical attributes between them became more and more different. For women, a large breast for breastfeeding and a wider pelvis were important for childbirth. Their arms and legs became narrower because they no longer had to do heavy physical labor to a large extent. For the men, strong arms and wider shoulders were important for hunting and fighting. A muscular rump and legs also indicated that they were physically well equipped for long-hunted marches. From our perspective today, women have become more and more feminine and men more and more masculine.

Their social behavior also changed. The women's priorities were food and children. For the men, it was hunting and fighting. Then they aligned their needs and desires as well as their decisions. Since both were of immense importance for survival, they had to influence and complement each other, which did not always go without problems, but ultimately led to further positive development. The equality of men and women became necessary for survival in the development of the human community.

But there was another problem in the tribe. By freely acting out their strong instincts, they have so far reproduced unchecked with everyone and everyone. So it came about that siblings, half-siblings, mothers, and sons as well as fathers and daughters fathered children together. Because of this, the proportion of stillbirths and freak births was high. Over the millennia, people recognized why it was and therefore avoided such connections.

That was a radical change in her sexual and social behavior. Free love in the family was indeed unbroken. But women could only have fun with their husbands and with each other. Outside the family, she was forbidden to have sex with men and of course with male family members. The man could not have any other wives either and outside the family could only have fun with men when they were hunting or just wanted to. This separation between families had a great advantage. By avoiding inbreeding, they no longer needed to have fresh blood from other strains to come to them. Because it was often associated with acts of war when they had to rob women.

The status of sexually mature children also changed fundamentally. They could no longer indulge in lust with the opposite sex. But only when they have started their own family. To do this, the young men had to look for a wife from another extended family.

Same-sex love was therefore a natural process also in this development phase. During the period of sexual maturity and before starting a family, the young people now enjoyed themselves almost exclusively for a relatively long time only as same-sex with each other. That was new. But even after they had started a family, the bisexual way of life was still interesting and appealing due to the greater physical and social differences between the sexes.

It can be assumed that this increased homosexuality, as some young people, who have now experienced this kind of pleasure full of joy for several years, wanted to stay with it. Especially since the physical difference between the sexes became more and more obvious and they preferred one type. But then there were also young people who, due to this increasing physical difference, later concentrated mainly on the opposite sex in their sexual fulfillment. Even at that time, it was a natural process in conscious individual sexual development. Most of them, however, then looked for the opposite sex to start a family and, because of their social ties from their youth, remained bisexual in their lust. Since everyone was under the protection of one family, they had to court a partner from another family. They did this by presenting themselves with jewelry and gifts, both men and women, and displaying their charms. They put more and more emphasis on the external appearance. That was new. During this time rituals between the sexes emerged, as they are still essentially performed today. However, based on their experiences, the decision was made by the heads of the families at that time. Because it was about the most important thing there was for them, namely to create the best conditions for reproduction and thus for the continued existence of the tribe.

After they decided to start a family, the couple had a trial period in this tribe, during which they lived together and could only live out their lust orally and anally. It gave them time to see how they got along and whether they can be happy with their partner. After all, they stayed together for the rest of their lives. Only when they got to know each other and made up their minds in favor of each other was the covenant made by the heads of the families.

This procedure is still used today in some indigenous peoples, as I experienced it myself in northern Thailand in the mountains.

There were six young men, between 14 and 16 years old, standing together and three girls of the same age eyed them curiously. At some point a girl ran to the boy she had chosen, talked to him for a while, and, when they agreed, they went away together and lived together for a probationary period of two to four weeks, as I was told. I asked what happens if the girl becomes pregnant during this time. I was told that this would not happen. You must not have sexual intercourse yet. But the older members of the clan have already trained them beforehand how they can still give each other a lot of pleasurable satisfaction.

As long as they are still alone and do not have a partner on trial, same-sex pleasure satisfaction is a matter of course. That was probably why the boy said goodbye to his friends before he left with the girl, as warmly as I could see. If they choose each other after the probationary period, the parents negotiate about it. When everything was settled, they eventually moved in together and started a family.

But I checked again and asked what would happen if the girl got pregnant and the two of them didn't get together. Because I couldn't imagine that something like that wouldn't happen. I was replied that the girl would then have to find another boy who would accept the child. Which wasn't a big problem either. It was common for them to take this trial period more often with different partners before deciding on one. There were also no set rules for a family. Sometimes a man and a woman lived alone, but sometimes a man lived with several women or vice versa.

That was based on what the gender ratio in the clan looked like at that time. So they had optimally adapted to the conditions in their seclusion.

In our story, too, they became a family and the man was free to take more wives as soon as he had fathered the first healthy child. Because with it he had proven his fertility and acquired the right to do so. It was therefore important that he correctly chose the first woman who was physically suitable for a likely healthy birth. Having several women also increased the responsibility to look after a larger family. In most cases, it was wanted by the women because it was beneficial for them. This way, they didn't have to do all the work alone and could split up childcare among themselves. They also had a lot of pleasurable fun together. Because the head of the family wasn't always with them because of the hunt. It wasn't a problem for him either, as he could have fun hunting with the other men. But it was unfavorable for the woman who was alone at home. To rule out any risks that she would eventually get involved with another man, the man was also interested in having at least a second woman in the house with whom she got along well.

Through the solid social coexistence in a large family and the free choice of partner, the emotional bond within the family became stronger. The love for one another grew. But it was not possessive and certainly not geared towards a monogamous relationship. People could love multiple people of either sex. That was the natural development in evolution.

In the extended family, women had a say in accepting a new member. Which the man was happy to accept because he wanted peace to reign in the family and the women to get along well. It also encouraged fun among them. So everyone was more balanced and satisfied. Today many men still have the fantasy of having pleasure with two or

33

more women at the same time. It probably originates from this time.

Tribal members who had chosen the same sex were equally respected in the clan. Same-sex men and women lived together in men's or women's shelters. Sometimes they were good mediators when it came to problems in the extended families. Some were gladly taken as medicine men. He didn't have time to start a family anyway. But medicine men were the most powerful and respected men in the tribe at the time. For same-sex lovers, there were no restrictions on their sexual passion. They could always and everywhere live out their lust in the women's or men's house or the individual extended families of the same sex. These men were mostly good craftsmen or artists and of course they liked to go hunting. The same-sex women cooked the meals together and helped with the children. But some also went hunting or became respected warriors. Like Eda. She was a muscular, strong woman and could throw the spear more accurately than anyone else. So she was very respected by the hunters and warriors. She lived in the women's shelter and was very popular with women there. But even in the extended families, the female members were very fond of her. So she became a role model for many women but also for the young men, who valued her for her skill in the hunt.

All lived out their great natural lust together, just as they felt and wanted it. For this period it can be assumed that bisexuality among women in the extended family developed more strongly. The relationship between the sexes, however, had changed fundamentally as a result of the selective selection that was now being made and the solid bonds that developed in an extended family. They continued to live bisexual, but only the men were polygamous in a family and with several women. Both sexes chose their partners and wooed them. This was new, and the different responsibilities in the family meant that social differences between men and women began to develop, but these were equated in terms of the position of the clan. This took place in a long evolutionary process in terms of further development. Due to their equal differences and the resulting conflicts of interest, there were always new impulses that contributed to the growth and development of people.

When analyzing historical developments, many amateurs and scientists conclude that positions of power between the sexes have always existed. Usually, it was the men, but sometimes the women too, who had the say. You can't prove that this was the case in the long term. They also derive these theories from evidence from the Stone Age, around 8000 years ago. Or they refer to the discovery of tribes that have so far hardly come into contact with civilization and where there are sometimes very hieratic relationships between the sexes. But even here we don't know how long it has been that way. These tribes also developed on their own or had contacts with other conquerors a long time ago. It is not even certain where they came from, maybe 20,000 years ago they were settled somewhere else and were influenced. But we are talking about a period of 100,000 years and more.

I think that these theories arise from today's false worldview, which is reflected in our consciousness and the conceptions and theories about the past that have developed from it. I cannot make friends with such theories. From my point of view, there is no logical reason why these gender fights should have existed at that time and under the conditions at that time. Perhaps there were a few exceptions, but they cannot be generalized. That would only have been bad for the living conditions of the hunters and gatherers.

On the contrary, man could only develop optimally because there was equality between the sexes and he was aware of that.

Gender inequality only arose with the emergence of private property, through social inequality. We'll get to that later.

36

Epilogue

This wild and unrestrained exercise of pleasure naturally served primarily to live out the joy and bliss that we also experience in it today. But she also created strong social and free, emotional connections between people, which contributed to their successful development and probably also personally to more joie de vivre. It was the longest period of development in human life so far, sexually and socially, by which we are still shaped today.

We too carry sexual diversity in our genes and our physical conditions. We feel it, have many fantasies and needs. Some let it rest or deny it. But others are also not aware of this and do not even know why they are so dissatisfied. Some go after them. Not only when living out their sexual bliss, but they don't just fall in love with one person. However, they have unfounded feelings of guilt or they are talked into them by another partner, which greatly limits their happiness. Yes, sometimes it even turns into the opposite. This not only destroys the happiness of others but also your own. I know examples from many real stories that men and women told me in my work. Few of them lead a really sexually and socially fulfilling life today.

2.3. The life of the arable farmers and ranchers

The people multiplied. Over time it became more and more difficult to kill enough game for food and to collect plants. Since the women were responsible for the preparation of the food in the extended family, they began to search for new sources of food. Likely, it was mainly they who started growing plants and raising pets to support their extended family. In doing so, they laid the foundation for the peaceful and finally settled society of arable farmers and ranchers.

Ami, a woman in her mid-thirties, was the head of her tribe. The human world began to change dramatically. They had finally settled down and were no longer hunters and gatherers, but cattle breeders and farmers. By farming, they now had a place where they could spend their whole life. It was worth building stronger huts. The craft developed. Coexistence and the division of labor were better organized. However, this made it more difficult for other groups to be accepted. Because there was common property in the form of fields (land) and cattle herds (pastures), which they could not and would not easily share with other strangers. Unless they brought something into the community that they needed or wanted. Even if it was communal property, it was a new form of property that was necessary to maintain and improve their living conditions. This also gave rise to an administration and the first script. Agriculture and animal husbandry were dependent on fertility. So came the age of the fertility cult. The women who gave birth were therefore just as revered and in some regions the leaders of their clan. There it was the women who headed the extended family in this community and usually had several male partners. The men gradually lost their function as hunters and warriors and became farmers and ranchers.

It was women who brought forth new life. This was a prerequisite for maintaining society and promised happiness and satisfaction. Whether in the fields, with the cattle, or in the family. Fertility was the guarantee for a good and successful life in prosperity and contentment. The women were therefore greatly admired by the men and raised by them to the position of head of the extended family. Nevertheless, they made the decisions together.

Women should have children with many men to carry on their genetic makeup in all their diversity. Here, too, sexual fulfillment was only possible within the extended family with the opposite sex in order not to endanger their functionality. That was the prerequisite for a stable society and its development for the benefit of all. The offspring they raised should come exclusively from the family and pass on their genetic makeup. It was the law, so they obeyed it, at least most of the time.

As equal members, the men had a say in a new male entry into the extended family. Or maybe they found a new husband to join the family themselves. After all, they too had to understand each other. During this time, the men within the extended family, but also outside, were enthusiastically active with one another. Physical development had created all the prerequisites for experiencing it with the greatest pleasure. And the women promoted it. As a result, the men were balanced and satisfied and not, as was usual and necessary in the past, aggressive and warlike. Because they didn't need that anymore.

In sedentary societies, it was important to regulate the birth rate. This is probably why polygamy was introduced. Just as it is still common today for this reason in some regions of the world. Of course, this required a considerable surplus of men when founding a sedentary group. In some regions, therefore, female offspring were killed immediately after birth. The killing of newborns was not uncommon. Malformed children, who used to be born primarily through inbreeding, were likely killed immediately after birth for thousands of years. It was a matter of survival and advancement at the time and cannot be measured by our standards today. Infanticide immediately after birth has been shown to have been carried out all over the world and has been a tradition for a long time, in some regions up to modern times, especially with newborn girls. However, new archaeological finds also indicate that there were long migrations by groups of women who were probably looking for a new clan or founded one in another location. In this way, they also spread knowledge and have thus become an engine of knowledge transfer.

Since the image of women was revered as an image of fearfulness, it is conceivable that during this time first the travesty and later the transsexuality emerged playfully in the men's house of same-sex love. Which was a special chance for the men in the extended family. In travesty, men like to take on the appearance of women. What had to be popular at that time? But these men were also quite active with the same sex, which the others liked too. Later, it probably often developed playfully within the extended families.

And although most women were sexually stressed with their husbands, they also met each other and did not want to miss the special, tender, lustful encounters with other women. Especially because in the extended family they were surrounded by an overhang of men. In this way, they could live out their great lustful instincts to the fullest in all ways, in a natural way. To pursue their same-sex sexual desire, no one was dependent on the extended family alone, and no one expected that. Social and emotional ties were certainly lived out in her but were not limited to that. A long period of peace began. There was no hunger in it, the craft developed, and everyone was essentially healthy and strong. As is shown by finds from this period.

If the children reached a sexually mature age, they had to start their own extended family. That was straightforward but new. The young man applied to a woman he liked. If she took a liking to him and the other men who might already be in the family, then he was accepted. The extended family he came from only had an advisory role, but no longer had a say. Only when the new man was allowed by the woman to have sexual intercourse with her so that it poured into her, as he accepted. Before that, both had the right to break the connection. So the tradition developed that a marriage is only valid if it has been sexually consummated. Which remained valid well beyond this development period and is still a tradition in many cultures today.

At that time Ina was just becoming sexually mature and preparing for a family of her own. How she was led, she had seen and learned from childhood in her family. Now a house had to be built for her, which her extended family took over. As a household of her own, she received, like everyone else, a share per person of the total yield of the harvest, the milk from the cattle and the meat. She just took it with her, because until now her extended family got it for her as long as she lived with them. The man she chose also brought an equal share from his family.

When the house was finished, the first young men came and wooed them. Among them were two friends who wanted to come to her together. That had several advantages. If a woman did not give birth after three years, then the man or men could break away from her. If two men started their household, the chance was greater that they would have a child sooner. Her household also received three shares, which was easier to divide.

During their decision-making phase, there was no coitus between them, but she could watch the two men playing lustful games to see if they were good lovers, because she too wanted to satisfy her strong lust in them later. However, one of the friends was a bit thin and looked very pale. She did not find that favorable for the youngsters. The other was a strong and handsome boy who she liked. But they just wanted to get together. So she got involved on a trial basis. The thinner one was a jewelry maker. She liked that again. He was very smart. When having sex with his boyfriend, he had more stamina and a bigger member than the other, which impressed her. His friend, on the other hand, was a real beauty. She realized that when she saw him standing so naked and noticed how he gave himself to his friend with pleasure. He was muscular and had a great bum. Overall, they complemented each other perfectly and she decided to take both. After watching the young men for ten days in their ecstatic lust, she couldn't take it anymore. She let them both in that day. The alliance was thus closed. Since they complemented each other so well, most of the time she was all three together. They had great joy and were happy with the decision. The pleasure of being together for three was varied and extremely ecstatic. They played this game a lot in the beginning because they were very young and full of energy and passion. Ina also wanted to get pregnant as soon as possible. After three months she was and was greatly admired by her two husbands.

During this time, a new form of advertising among the sexes developed, the form still dominant today, that it is the task of men to advertise a woman. Women are adored and adored in advertising. However, this is usually not permanent in our day and age.

The time of the arable farmers and ranchers was peaceful. Nobody had to go hungry and a certain amount of prosperity developed. Not all people were needed to get food. In this way, the craft and art could also develop more quickly. They got an equal share of the income. At that time there were also social facilities such as baths. In the beginning, there was no trade in goods or there was only very limited trade with outsiders.

The progressive division of labor developed a further specialization and people were able to develop differently due to their gifts, talents, and intellect. Since the time of hunters and gatherers was over, after the selection of suitable partners was mainly based on physical attributes, a more differentiated partner selection was now also possible according to character and intelligence.

Women were revered in their role as mothers, but they also took part in the division of labor on an equal footing. They worked in the fields and raised livestock. Gender equality was thus also balanced in the division of labor. Due to the prevailing bisexuality, it was not a problem in sexual freedom when women had more men. Couples were also free to start a family for two. But what happened very rarely in the long run due to the polygamous natural way of life. It was possible to bring more partners into the extended family at any time. Couples who wanted to enjoy their togetherness could do so until they decided on a change.

There were no differences in the division of wealth in this society. This was therefore of no importance when choosing a partner. It was a self-contained, harmonious, and peaceful society in which people lived relatively contentedly and happily. They were free to live out their sexual desire except for a necessary restriction. As long as no one entered this social system by force. They did not know war and conquests and so for a long time, they saw no reason to protect themselves from intruders.

Epilogue

This epoch created a more colorful and therefore more interesting life in sexual pleasure and fulfillment. Feelings of affection and love were omnipresent in all their diversity. There were contentment, happiness, and peace. This variety of sexual pleasure is still there today and has become even more diverse. Only in our time, the individual groups set themselves apart from one another, whereas at the time of the arable farmers and cattle breeders they were lived out by everyone in their own sexual life, right up to the extended family. This led to more joie de vivre and satisfaction.

If we put aside our prejudices to recognize that we could live out these possibilities in all their diversity today without remorse or feelings of guilt, if we wanted to, makes us free and happier. You don't need a lot of imagination to realize how much more joy it would offer us today.

There are still many-man marriages (polyandry) with a woman today. Besides, Wikipedia: Polyandric societies can still be found today in parts of India, in the Himalayas (Tibet, Kashmir, Himachal Pradesh, Sikkim), in Bhutan, in the Congo, in northern Nigeria, and among the Paviotso (North America), Marquesas and the Da-La (Indochina), in antiquity also in Sparta, like Xenophon, Polybios, Plutarch and Nikolaos Damaskenos attest.

In this period of development, however, other decisive changes affect us today in a much more pronounced form. So it was important to know when the grain had to be sown and harvested. When the cattle should best be covered, you had to pay attention to the weather and much more. In other words, time played an increasingly important role. That was new because the word time didn't even exist before. People lived timelessly and just did what was necessary or when they felt like it. But now they were often pressed for time. That more or less shaped their social life. Today time plays an enormous role in our lives. We are often under time pressure. Sometimes this is so dominant that social relationships are severely disturbed and with it our pleasurable and social relationships. Much remains non-binding. Many people today believe that they have no time to build a stable social relationship and therefore satisfy themselves with quick impersonal sex or themselves. I know this from many conversations with clients or in groups. Such an attitude certainly keeps us from a permanently fulfilled, lustful, and happy life and thus disrupts our evolutionary development.

With the right life concepts, we would certainly be able to regain a lot of time for ourselves and our happiness today. More on that later.

2.4. The lustful relationship of people with nature and animals

Back then, in the days of agriculture and animal husbandry, people had a completely different relationship to nature than they do today. They did not feel superior to her, but one with them and were grateful for a good harvest. This is why the harvest festival is still celebrated in many regions today. This custom was adopted by the Church because it suited their beliefs, but it is thousands of years older.

At that time they believed (or knew) that plants, and especially trees, have a soul, and naturally enjoyed themselves with them. Today, hugging the trees is back in fashion and many feel the tremendous power and energy flowing within them. An emotional connection with nature is created.

When I once held a management seminar lasting several days at my institute at the time, I took the participants to the meadow in front of the house on the first morning. They looked at me questioningly, still tired. I asked them to find a tree and hug it. They should develop a personal relationship with their favorite tree to get a closer connection with nature. During her stay with me, that became an everyday morning ritual. It also happened that some members came to the seminar too late, with the excuse "My tree did not let go of me so quickly." Of course, I did not ask any further questions.

Lustful feelings were part of the attitude towards life back then. They were nothing special and were not suppressed or marginalized. In a time of being one with nature and the free development of pleasure, this naturally led to ecstatic encounters and trees are the ideal partners for this.

But animals played a special role. People did not put themselves above them, but sometimes even saw them as superior and therefore adored them. When they had to kill animals to survive, they thanked them for their help and were firmly convinced that they too had an immortal soul. Finds from this period prove this.

Animals were equal to humans and they attributed a high level of intelligence and special positive qualities to them. Some were domesticated at the time and people were with them all day. Often they lived with them under one roof. They also saw and felt her sexual arousal. Sometimes they shared it with them. There are also reliefs and stone age wall paintings showing people with animals during sexual union. Certainly, it was not just a matter of pure pleasure satisfaction. Rather, it shows the deep connection between the people of that time and them.

That was the beginning of what is known as sodomy, which is still practiced today. In the past, it was mostly farm animals such as goats and sheep with whom they experienced this bond, in our time it is mainly domestic animals such as dogs that are preferred. One can assume that this happened frequently in the past and that there were also longer relationships between a person and an animal.

Today we can still see in our children the strong emotional bond they can build with their pets. How intense must this connection have been at a time when there was a much stronger relationship with nature and animals? Especially when they often spent the whole day alone with them in a pasture.

Understandably, the first depictions of creatures that were half-human and half-animal also date from this time. Usually, they are stronger and smarter than humans. They combined with the strong characteristics of an animal that was superior to him in some way. These human-animal-beings then pull themselves through all historical epochs. The best known is probably the Sphinx in Egypt. But there are countless other representations as well.

The widespread ones are:
- Centaur (half-horse, half-human)
- Pan the Shepherd God (with the lower body of a ram or a billy goat)
- Minotaur (a being with a human body and a bull's head)

Epilogue

Sex with animals is a big taboo topic in our day and age. Nevertheless, there is still a lot of love and emotional connection to them in people today. If you have open and trusting conversations on this topic, you may be amazed at how many people can imagine pleasurable experiences with an animal.

In this context, I once had an experience with my dog myself.

Since I often write late into the night, I sometimes lay down on the sofa after lunch and fell asleep for 10 to 15 minutes. But I couldn't sleep any longer, because then it became too much for my dog, a cute little miniature schnauzer male. He then jumped on the sofa and stood with his four paws on my chest and stomach. I woke up and he looked at me expectantly. I should get up and go out with him. Once I didn't feel like getting up. I said sleepily: "Come on, I'll give you a bioenergetic back massage." Up until then I only used it in my work. Then I massaged his back and closed my eyes again. When I looked at him a little later, I noticed that he had gotten an erection and was standing motionless on my chest. I looked at him amused and said: "Well, you seem to like that." He immediately jumped off me. My tone must have put him off. In any case, it didn't happen to him again, although from then on he liked to enjoy a massage from me.

Sex with animals has always existed and still is today. Even if it was certainly never the rule in earlier times, it was accepted and recorded in art. Thanks to the Internet, more and more people are reporting about their personal sexual experiences with animals. So it does not seem to have died out in our time either, although there are no reliable studies on it. And in my opinion, it doesn't necessarily have to give.

It was only important for me to show the historical development up to today and the reasons for it.

Of course, in the time of the "social market economy", a business was made out of it again and animals were trained and rented out directly for them. There are also enough porn films of it. The fact that there are customers for this only shows once more that free sexual development is disturbed in our time in social coexistence, and in this case also has absolutely nothing to do with the natural, pleasurable relationships between people and loved animals.

Incidentally, the Bible has pronounced its ban on this and says: "Furthermore, if a man mates with an animal, he shall be infallibly punished with death, and you shall also kill the animal." (Leviticus chapter 20, verse 15; Quantity Bible, 1939) and elsewhere: "You may not mate with any animal and thereby defile yourself, and a female person may not stand in front of an animal to be mated by it; that would be a shameful sin. "(Leviticus / Leviticus chapter 18, verse 23; the multitude of Bible, 1939).

So if the Bible writes about it so extensively, then it was probably not that unusual at the time, and yet it was common.

In Germany too, according to the Animal Welfare Act, it is forbidden to "use an animal for one's sexual activities…" Violations of the prohibition can be punished with a fine of up to 25,000 euros. I don't understand how animal rights activists, who should have a particularly deep understanding and knowledge of animals, assume that humans "use" these animals in any case. I think you cannot always assume that there has been sexual abuse of animals in general. Against this, people have complained to the Constitutional Court. The lawsuit was denied. Probably because the animal could not credibly confirm that it happened by mutual agreement.

3. The redistribution of the world and the end of social and sexual equality between the sexes

Unfortunately, the era of arable farmers and ranchers lasted only a few thousand years in peace and prosperity. Then it was replaced by wars and conquests. For the first time, prosperity arose, which has always been a powerful motive for the destruction of cultures by people who did not have it but wanted to have it.

Agriculture and cattle breeding remained, but the land that was the previously common property was now owned by a single conqueror. Everything depended on owning the land. Who secured agriculture and the pastures for the animals? The prosperity that arose from it belonged to whoever declared the land his property through military might. The only thing left to do with ordinary people was to serve them. Whereby the rule was exercised very differently at that time. It went from large families and communities that lived well in this system to total exploitation, impoverishment, and enslavement of the people. Trade flourished as a result of the further specialization that went with it and the increasing surplus of production, which was no longer distributed equally. This created a wealthy middle class. This, in turn, was the engine of an economic upswing at the expense of increasing poverty.

The sexual pleasure remained unbroken and for most people, it was the only happiness they had in their poverty. Since there were now rich and poor, that was probably the beginning of prostitution for women and men. It wasn't the oldest trade in the world, but it was one that anyone could easily do. Certainly often out of necessity. Offering sex and lust for food or a better life by the side of a richer man or woman was something completely new and the beginning of leading natural happy lust down a wrong, destructive path.

Sexual pleasure and ecstasy have been shown to influence our soul, outside of the reproductive instinct, or, as the psychologist would say, the psyche. You have to be free from any coercion or other motives to receive the happiness in life and the unique joy in it, in which mind, soul, and body develop. Therefore they can only find their actual fulfillment with people in a socially familiar environment, with the sole motive of affection and trust. Which, of course, can sometimes happen very quickly and at short notice, but should not be associated with any kind of consideration. From this point of view, a pleasurable, honest relationship with an animal or tree was even more honest and mentally profitable at this point in human development.

There were also more and more gods who demanded sexual acts. The young women and men were taken care of when they joined the cult, and in return gave their bodies for ecstatic and orgasmic games. This type of sexual activity did not create a social bond and was directed against evolutionary development. In those days they were mostly consecrated to the gods, but only the priests and the guests they invited received from them. The young women and men who had to make themselves available were mostly only used. They could not even live out their sexuality with relish, but only did what he was told. Sometimes even by believing in the gods with full devotion. So prostitution under the guise of religious fanatics at a high level. Sometimes it still exists in some sects today.

Some cults were virgins and youths were supposed to be untouched in honor of the gods. It was unnatural torture for those affected. There are still millions of that in the Catholic Church today. Ultimately, because of the ever-increasing wealth, it was about the question of power. Priests and cults were not only promoted by rulers but also believed in them themselves. So the priests gained power over them. And the people were pacified. Karl Marx once said: "Religion is opium for the people." And it was the same. Rules could be drawn up, which everyone then followed in their blind faith. The ruler himself became a god and inviolable. Cults, in which the strongest instincts of the people were addressed, namely sex, were very effective and were thus promoted. Sex became a commodity and an advertising magnet. All of this has nothing to do with fulfilled and natural pleasure.

But how did people live out their sexual lust?

While sex previously played an important role in the cohesion of a group, it is now gradually losing its social significance. With the introduction of private property, social life was also regulated by norms and laws established by a small ruling group. There were several strata of the population, which were subdivided according to their private property. The right of inheritance to property resulted in marriages intended to secure or expand the social status of a class. That then often had nothing to do with connections in lustful love.

Sex was either violently taken, blackmailed, or bought by the wealthier classes. It was often offered by the lower classes specifically for a better life. Today we still know the saying: "Success makes you sexy." This means nothing else that successful people can usually offer one or more partners a secure and materially good life. The natural free and unrestrained sexual pleasure was ended. They only existed in the undiscovered primitive peoples. That was anything but an advance in the development of evolution. There was wild and spontaneous sex, also and especially among the poorer population, but it was mainly drive-

driven and no longer had any great social significance. At most in the form of religious folk festivals in which an ecstatic coexistence of groups of people took place.

Bisexuality was also largely used for personal interests. But it also gained a completely different meaning. If it had previously been lived out freely and on an equal footing and thus had an important function for a happy and socially bound life in the group, it became a necessity for sexual satisfaction over long periods due to the mass, long separation of the sexes. That was natural, but here too the social function often played a subordinate role.

This long separation was mainly caused by wars of conquest. Large armies such as in the Roman Empire, with Alexander the Great, Hannibal, in the Orient and Asia, often separated the sexes for many years. The sexual pleasure, however, remained and was lived out as one-sex with one another. Alexander the Great had almost 50,000 men in his army who had not seen a woman for many years. The army in the Roman Empire even comprised a strength of 250,000 to 300,000 men. They too were among themselves for years. It is estimated that there were still more than 300,000 gladiators during the time of the Roman Empire, who also hardly saw any women. And so it can be observed all over the world at this time.

But it was not only through wars of conquest that there was a long separation between the sexes. Also and above all through building work by the rulers. For example, it took 6,700 men to build the great pyramid for twenty years. More than 20 million men worked on the construction of the Great Wall in China for more than 300 years. Lately, they have allowed families in the labor camp, but there has been a great shortage of women. All over the world, there was huge and long-lasting construction that resulted in a separation of the sexes or at least an imbalance.

Due to the mass separation and the mass killings of the soldiers in the battles they had to fight, the women had too few men. Natural bisexuality was overworked by the lack of opportunities and no longer conformed to the evolutionary laws of free sexual development. The ruling class, which did not have to witness these separations, blackmailed and bought them, like sex in general. Since bisexuality was present everywhere in the empire at that time due to the long mass divisions, it was also abundantly lived out in the ruling class. It is believed that in Egypt, for example, same-sex love was part of the development of young nobles. High cultures like ancient Greece lived it freely and extensively with relish without any deficiency.

Epilogue

The relationship between the sexes changed demonstrably abruptly and later finally with the stipulation in the Old Testament: "The wife is subject to the husband." (Colossians 3:18 "You women, be subject to your husbands in the Lord, as it is due. ") About 3000 years ago. And no matter how it is interpreted today: This is exactly how it was practiced for thousands of years. It was not until the twentieth century, for example, that women could vote.

Here is another biblical text: 1 Corinthians 14:34

"As in all the churches of the saints, keep your wives silent in the church; for they should not be allowed to speak, but should be subject, as the law also says. "

For a long time, an internal and external battle between the sexes began, which is not yet over and which had a devastating effect on the evolutionary development of man. Even today, gender equality in society is not in sight. Mainly because nobody understands what equality or equal rights should look like in the competitive society in which we live today? People, men, and women alike disagree on this and sometimes it bears ridiculous style blooms. Of course, this has consequences for sexual fulfillment in our time.

Everyone should find their way here. This affects both sexes. The equality that has been suppressed for so long must mainly come from within. You shouldn't rely on laws, quota regulations, the media, and the like or allow yourself to be influenced. It only shows the helplessness of the social leaders to recognize the problem: namely the wrong way of life that is imposed on us by the prevailing social and economic rules and laws. But to change that, you have to rethink it thoroughly. That is why you find your happiness in the family, whatever the division of labor, or in a social group into which you want to integrate. Gender equality is easy to implement there because it is like human coexistence.

Only there you can create the basis under today's conditions and build a happy and fulfilling life for yourself. Is it really important what you do or is it important that you find your fulfillment in what you do and that this is recognized equally in the family or a group? So do you receive appreciation for it and take an equal position in decisions? As I said, this applies to both men and women. You will not be happy in a fateful achievement society as it is currently dominant with its manipulative ideology and the market economy.

Men and women have evolutionarily linked in a very natural way inequality. Even that is still in the genes today. If they do not allow themselves to be influenced from outside, they will feel and be able to live this mutual respect and respect for one another. Use your different ways of thinking to develop yourself further in this avoidable contradiction between man and woman and to become happier. A very important role is played by your tolerance and the lustful behavior towards each other, which will help you a lot to grow together with your differences. Sexual development stagnated during this period under the conditions of private property and the emergence of strong social differences between rich and poor. Although these differences still exist today, they are no longer as pronounced, at least in the developed industrial countries. Especially since in most cases, even in the lower classes, there is no longer any direct need. Totalitarian violence no longer exists in many countries today, and therefore also no longer has the power to legally satisfy sexual needs by force. We have a certain amount of self-determination, including our bodies and our sexual activities. But there are still many prejudices, even within us, sometimes wrong beliefs.

We have had the freedom to enjoy sexual pleasure and love for hundreds of thousands of years. Now we have to fight for it again, also within ourselves. We have partially succeeded in doing this in many regions of the world. It is a chance or a prerequisite to regaining our full freedom in the most beautiful thing in the world. The living conditions give the green light for this. To do this, we not only have to fight to change rules and laws but also change our prejudices and false beliefs. And that's a lot more difficult. We should recognize that these prejudices and beliefs, to which we were helplessly exposed as children, are directed against ourselves and hinder us in our sexually pleasurable and wonderful fulfillment. A process that allows us to grow and make us happy.

There is more and more frustration, feelings of guilt, and anonymous orgasmic experiences that serve the short-term satisfaction, instead of felt, socially bound pleasure fulfillment. Our natural and existing mental and physical prerequisites for a happy social life in free sexual pleasure are a chance to break the chains that were put on us around 3000 years ago by social rules and norms. In the next chapter, you will find out what really happened back then and how it still affects us today.

4. The dramatic aberration and the social and sexual oppression of religious teachings

Everything changed about 3000 years ago, with the Old and then with the New Testament, which is still called the foundation of the Catholic Church today. People were put in an unnatural straitjacket, especially when it came to their natural sexual needs. But she did not want to or could not accept that. Here are some examples:

In the wealthy class, young girls were disguised as servants and pleasure boys as servants or squires. The main motive behind it, however, was the pleasurable pleasure with them. The slave trade of young women and youths flourished because slaves had no rights and in this social status could be used unrestrainedly for the satisfaction of sexual pleasure. It was so present that today some people also playfully use it to satisfy their lust, and violence often plays a pleasurable role in this.

Whore houses were springing up like mushrooms, especially in the cities. There is also that today. None of this ended before the institutions of the Church either.

The forced unnatural abstinence led to mass whoring. And that was a perfectly normal reaction. The common people continued to celebrate pagan festivals, where a large group of people unrestrainedly indulged their lust. Such festivals were also held at ruling houses, as the story of Solomon and the Queen of Sheba shows, for example. Sex was dissolute wherever possible under the guise of pagan religious festivals. People needed an outlet to live out their pent-up natural lust.

Even for poor people, there were whores and men who could no longer sell themselves dearly. And they were gladly accepted by the poor.

61

Bisexuality continued to exist. But nowhere near as it would have been natural. The poor people in particular were afraid of it. Didn't they keep hearing about the terrible punishments of God in church when they lived out their lust? Many poor and ignorant people then believed in it. So this lustful side of her life was nailed up. While at the same time the pastor who was preaching this to them was enjoying himself with relish with his acolyte. There are very likely tens of thousands of cases in the world today. And that was and still is in the highest circles of the Church. Even high dignitaries enjoyed themselves with young priests and women. Which was quite natural. Only the mendacity and the false rules that they imposed on people under high threat of punishment were devastating. The dramatic consequences of this huge lie of the Church can no longer be fully grasped. It can be assumed that millions of people were killed as a result of this in the course of history. And today there is still the death penalty for infidelity and same-sex love in some countries.

So Michael was walking along a dirt road on a beautiful summer day. He was 23 years old and grew up in a monastery. He got his first orgasm when friars in the monastery, who came to the boys' dormitory every night, stroked his aroused member. That was exciting, and although he knew it was strictly forbidden, he was happy to let it. It was the friars who did it. So it had to be godly. Since the abbot of the monastery also took a liking to him, he was very fortunate that he was promoted by him. He learned the pastor's office in the monastery and had now got his first congregation. It was only a small village, but he was proud to finally have his community. The separation from the monastery was not difficult for him. Full of ideas and joy, he now ran to his village. He was eagerly awaited there because they hadn't had a pastor for two years. His first sermon was well received by the people. And since he was very friendly, he quickly became popular in this small town. One day a boy came up to him and said that he had seen another boy let a man mount him. So he called the sinner and confronted him. Of course, he denied everything because he knew the severe punishment that would await him. He was 15 years old and a strikingly handsome young man. The pastor suggested that he be his altar boy. That way he could keep an eye on him better. He said. He wanted to refrain from punishment. The boy beamed at him gratefully and of course, immediately agreed. He carried out his duties in the church conscientiously and adored his pastor. One day, the sermon had just ended and the church was empty, they both ran into the backroom to take off their church clothes. He saw his acolyte grow restless, and he knew why. For a long time, it had been a matter of indifference to him when they stood together while undressing. He looked at his acolyte when he had taken off his robe. Then he noticed its stiff member. Now he couldn't hold back either. They hugged and rubbed their bodies together. Then they undressed and the boy turned and bent down. After that, everything went its natural course. The lustful moans showed how much they both enjoyed. He too wanted to experience the pleasure he had given the boy because he already knew him from the monastery, and he bent down too. And his acolyte did his work full of enthusiasm. After they finished they dressed without saying a word, and a little later he was alone in the church. Now the guilt gripped him. He was the parish priest, something like that was not allowed to happen.

So he took an eight-strand leather whip and ran to the altar. There he exposed his back and flogged himself in remorse. He had to show repentance or he wouldn't go to heaven. Feeling great guilt, he whipped himself so hard that the blood came to him. Then he lay on his stomach in front of the altar and asked God for forgiveness. At dinner that evening, he was convinced that something like this would never happen again.

The next day he visited some parishioners. On the street, he met his acolyte who greeted him warmly. He told him to come to church the next day to clean the altar. The boy beamed at him and said yes. When he ran back to church, he thought of him and saw the pictures before him, how he had given himself to it with relish the day before. Now he was looking forward to the next meeting.

What a nice happy ending, you should believe. Only at that time, it was punished with imprisonment and hellfire. And so it is still today.

What did the major religions accomplish in the sexual fulfillment of people during this time? Let's summarize the most important rules from the Old and New Testament:

Sex can only take place in a marriage between a man and a woman.

As it is said:

> ➢ You shall not commit adultery. (The sixth commandment) For a while, this sex was only allowed to take place in some religious directions to procreate children. So it was only the reproductive instinct that was allowed. That wasn't the rule even in the animal kingdom. This is how the ideology of the church arose that it had to look after its flocks.

> ➢ Sex outside of marriage was forbidden. Yes, even the thought of it was forbidden. As it is said: "You shall not covet your neighbor's wife, servant, maid, cattle or anything that is his." (The tenth

commandment) or Matt. 5, 27-28: Jesus says: "You have heard that it is said: You shall not commit adultery. But I tell you that everyone who looks at a woman to lust for her has already committed adultery with her in his heart. "

➤ Masturbation was forbidden because indulging in physical desire outside of marriage, in whatever form, is a sin.

Same-sex love was forbidden. Here is a Bible text from many about it: Lev 18.22 EU: "You should not lie with a man as you do with a woman; it is an abomination. "In another Bible text, there is also the death penalty for it.

Sex with animals is prohibited. The divine punishment for sodomy was death: (repetition) "Furthermore, if a man mates with an animal, he shall be infallibly punished with death, and you shall also kill the animal" (Leviticus chapter 20), Verse 15; set of Bible, 1939)

What does that tell us? But first of all, mainly that all of this has always existed before. And not only in secret or rarely, then it would certainly not have been named publicly in such writings, but at some point, it was part of the natural sexual fulfillment of people. The church then only "demonized" it.

That means in plain language that all sexually mature people were not allowed to have any pleasurable encounters, not even with themselves. Yes, they weren't even allowed to think about it. It was only allowed in a marriage that at that time could only be concluded by the Church. For a while, sex was supposed to be removed from people's thoughts and feelings and was seen only as a necessary evil in having children. At least according to the teachings of the Church. That was against nature and all reason. Although some in the scriptures also praised married sex, it did not prevail for a long time. Humans should develop back sexually, where only the reproductive motives counted.

Here is a matching Bible text:

Then God said: "Now we want to make people, an image of ourselves that is similar to us [...]." So God created people in his image, in God's image he created them and created them as men and women. And God blessed the people and said to them: "Be fruitful and multiply! Fill the whole earth and take possession of it! […]. "So it happened. And God looked at everything that he had created and saw that it was all very good. (Genesis 1: 26-31)

At that time, however, humans had long since developed much more sexually and socially. The diversity of sexual and social functions that fulfilled life and happiness was simply denied, demonized, and strictly forbidden. But that had nothing to do with morality, it was power interests. They wanted to gain absolute control over people. It was a step backward over hundreds of thousands of years.

How could such a religion even prevail among people?

Everything that was forbidden and demonized was quite normal at that time and was part of life and contributed to our development for hundreds of thousands of years. Did people realize that they were happy with it for 300,000 years but lived wrongly? Was that why they were glad that someone finally came to tell them?

Hardly likely. No, but for one thing, they couldn't read the Bible themselves. On the other hand, this religion was revolutionary through the preaching of charity and was by far the best means for the ruling class to consolidate its power. They recognized that. Not all of them immediately, but most of them within a short period. So it was promoted by them. There were three main reasons for this.

1. I am the Lord your God. Thou shalt have no other gods before me. (First commandment)
Before that, the ruling class had to come to terms with many gods. So many priests influenced the people. They all had to be satisfied. As a result, there were more unrest and power struggles among the various faiths at that time. A single God, whom everyone worshiped, came at just the right time. So they only had one religion and its representatives with whom they had to agree. At that time they were sure of their leadership role in the country. Little did they know that a single religion can usurp enormous power for a people? Later this religion, at the zenith of its power, brought down great kings and emperors.

2. There were worldly leaders by God's grace. Therefore, they had to be obeyed.
What could be better for a secular ruler? Now he was able to demand obedience from all of his subjects through the only religion that existed because he had God's grace for it.

3. First Letter of John: "And this is the testimony that God has given us eternal life, and that life is in his Son. He who has the Son has life; he who does not have the Son of God does not have life. I wrote this to you so that you might know that you who believe in the name of the Son of God will have eternal life. "

There are still many biblical texts on eternal life and, above all, on paradise, to which believers go after death if they live according to the church's teachings. This religion promised the kingdom of heaven to all who obeyed the rules of the church. What a great joy it was for the ruler. After all, it says: "Only do everything obediently what the ruler charges you, for he has been chosen by the grace of God. The worse it is for you, the better it will be for you in paradise. Because paradise belongs to you. "This is exactly how the Church preached it at that time. There couldn't be a better system of exploitation.

Here is an excerpt from the Bible: "Happy are you poor, for yours is the kingdom of God" (Luke 6:20).

With such a unique and fantastic instrument of power that they had with the teachings at this time, the rulers paid for something to make this religion a permanent state religion. Houses of worship grew like mushrooms out of the ground next to the whorehouses already mentioned. The Word of God was being taught there every week. Everyone was required to join the Church. That was something completely new. Church teachings were already taught to the children. That was also new. This religion had to be in the minds of all people to finally and forever consolidate the power of the rulers. It became mankind's greatest instrument of exploitation. Some Church officials did it very thoroughly and ruthlessly. Others only half-heartedly because they did not stick to what they had to preach.

But what about sex?

That wasn't a problem. In any case, the ruling class did not obey the many prohibitions. And that was tolerated by the church, at least until the 13th century. Until then, polygamy was also a common practice in the ruling class. But otherwise, a joyful life was led with women, men, and boys. Most of the church people did too. Even popes demonstrably enjoyed themselves unrestrainedly with women and youths.

But the people diligently ran to church every week and were occasionally observed by their priest and visited when necessary to consolidate ecclesiastical and secular obedience. The social and sexual repression through marriage became a permanent fixture there. The children also had their church education. And prejudices and false beliefs that were implanted in childhood are particularly strong in people's consciousness. You already knew that back then.

At first, the common people secretly lived out their sexual desires, but then less often because of fear, as there were more and more informers and punishments became more frequent. So they started to believe in it. From this, from generation to generation, increasingly solid beliefs developed that were directed against their own needs and feelings. So marriage became more important to her. Because only there they could more or less live out their sexual pleasure. These beliefs are still anchored in us today. But once again clearly and unequivocally: From the beginning, marriage was only propagated as the most fundamental and therefore most important instrument of power of the church to dominate people socially and sexually. From then on, the church alone could determine whether or not to marry. It was still the only way people could indulge their naturally strong sexual lust. The church decided whether to bring people together for it. She only did that when they came to church diligently and were God-fearing.

And the many sexual prohibitions (especially bisexual love, which was still widespread at the time) served to ensure that nothing was allowed outside of marriage where people could of course have lived out their lives, but which also prevented uncontrolled strong social contacts. So they made it controllable for the church.

The church representatives only had to look after their "sheep" and make sure that everyone adhered to them. Marriage became a humanly deeply undignified instrument of exercise of power and led to stagnation and devolution. The free feelings of love were brutally suppressed and only steered into the channels that served the church. At no time did it correspond to the natural evolutionary development of man and it does not do so as long as it still exists as the "foundation" of society, even today.

One could argue now that marriage existed before. But these marriages arose out of necessity and not because it was human nature. Accordingly, they were not subject to so many prohibitions and rules. Due to the unjust distribution of social wealth, most of them could simply no longer afford an extended family, but they were also not monogamous and heterosexual. On the contrary, at that time same-sex relationships were socially recognized in some high cultures alongside marriage. At that time, there were still a lot of wives and a rich culture of same-sex relationships among the rich.

This marriage that the Church instituted was something entirely different. It should guarantee her absolute social and, necessarily, sexual control over people. The social development of the people was severely disrupted as a result. People became more selfish and often fought each other among and between families instead of supporting each other in pleasurable get-togethers. And that is partly still the case today, which is proven by many neighbors' liability disputes, inheritance disputes, and much more.

It was not until the end of the 13th century that the church had consolidated its power to such an extent that it could also impose its sexual rules on secular rulers. At least what came out. Polygamy was forbidden for them too and the marriage was concluded for life. What the ruler then did unofficially did not matter. The satisfaction of sexual pleasure with women, men, or boys was abundant in the church itself at all times. Nevertheless, it now had more power over the ruling class, which is often used in later historical developments.

Epilogue

I would like to confess at this point:

"I believe that evolution is based on an overarching, universal plan. But only consciousness can plan. Yes, I too believe in a higher universal consciousness from which I come, with which I can communicate and which I return to when my physical time here is over. But this "God" would never set up rules and norms by which people must conform. This contradicts the universal advancement he strives for. Because my "God" or the universal consciousness, of which I am a part, wants to come to new knowledge again and again through the undisturbed development of the imperfect person and grow himself in the process. However, it can help us to fulfill our desires in this life, which contributes to the growth of all. As I described it in my book: "Happiness is not a coincidence". But it will never dictate how a man should live.

We are imperfect and that is by design. "God" loves us all in our imperfections and that is exactly how he needs us. We don't need anyone to tell us in "God's name" what we can and cannot do. We have to learn and develop from ourselves and our experiences. This is the only way to grow growth in "God" or the universal order. Evolution shows us the way. This is especially true for the development of our wonderful sexual powers. It is an instrument of evolution that should move us forward. Nobody knows what importance it will have on the development of our consciousness in the future and where it will lead us.

Rules and norms in sexual development hinder us and are only raised by ignorant and imperfect people and often in "God's name". Some rules are demonstrably unnatural and are directed against evolution. And it should certainly not be adopted by society. No one can speak in "God's name". In its deliberate imperfection, it is incapable of doing this. And certainly not questionable fonts that were simply put together like that.

So I respect and share the belief in higher consciousness, some say God about it. Most people today belong to a religion and thus thank the creation from which everything arises. This gratitude is a great motivation for respect for life in general and can be decisive for one of the greatest challenges of our time, the preservation of our living space. Most religions today strive for love, peace, mercy, and mutual help, the most important qualities for a happy coexistence of people. Let us also not forget that it was the Protestant pastors who recognized same-sex love as equal before God, because for them only love counted. Only later did the company reluctantly follow suit. Many Christian youth groups today are also grappling with progressive thoughts about sexuality.

This and much more are very positive impulses for the further evolutionary development of humans and the world. There are also Christian currents and churches where these rules no longer exist. There God is love and is lived that way. Your highest goal is to unite all people through love, regardless of what religion they belong to and whether at all. All people are equal and nothing is prescribed to them. This has nothing to do with the nonsense that began around 3000 years ago and most of the negative consequences of it.

Certainly, there are people who, because of their deep faith or their spiritual gifts, can establish a stronger connection with "God" or, as I call it, with the universal consciousness. But this information, which they get mainly through feelings, is not suitable for establishing rules and norms for people. That in turn only arises from their little consciousness, which is imperfect and flawed.

And that began with the constitution and the latter interpretation and sorting out of the Old and New Testaments and was continued on and on. But nobody knows how these writings originally came about. How on earth can such a script, written and sorted out by human hands, be made into such an eternally valid dogma? So the prohibitions and rules on human sexual behavior came from them and not from God. And they are wrong.

God would never make rules and prohibitions about human sexual development. On the contrary, in my opinion, it goes against his divine or evolutionary plan. Such false prohibitions and commandments, however, were adopted by society, which developed rules, "moral" norms and laws from them, which are directed against the free development of human beings and which today still give a false and distorted picture of it, no matter how avoidably progressive also some countries want to deal with it.

Even a Pope like Francis still talks about sin today when there is same-sex love. And it gets even worse! He believes that you can still re-educate children in whom you notice homosexual tendencies. That made me so sad. The word "sin" is also a word that the Church has invented. Sin is one of the greatest nonsense in world history. Finally, get rid of it.

And he thinks that only man and woman are a family in the image of God. What then: "Does God have a wife? If not, why is the marriage of man and woman an image of God? Why marriage at all? Who said that? Did God tell Francis personally, or did it only come from questionable writings selected for this purpose, which incidentally also constantly contradict each other? On the one hand, same-sex love is a mortal sin, on the other hand, among many other examples, there is:

King David said in the book of 2 Samuel 1 to his beloved Jonathan: "Your love for me was more wonderful than the love of women". Or to avoid misunderstandings, the repetition: 2 Sam 1.26 EU: "Woe to me for you, my brother Jonathan. You were very dear to me. Your love for me was more wonderful than the love of women. "Incidentally, David also had eight main wives. Funny, everyone was allowed to, only the common people were domesticated sexually monogamous.

Or did Jesus have a wife? No, he had twelve men around him day and night for many years. And they had built a strong social bond with each other. What did they do with their lusts that night? I don't know. But the question is legitimate.

The most common, if any, the response I received was that they were connected in deep faith. How so? Did you see Jesus and immediately had a deep faith in one another? Hardly likely. This is even portrayed differently in the Bible. But it is written that Jesus had a favorite disciple, John. Time and again the Bible writes about John: "The disciple whom Jesus loves ..." (I Jn 13: 21-30). Why do you do that? Jesus loved all people and his disciples especially. So why the clear reference to John?

Columbia University historian Morton Smith reviewed an early manuscript of the Gospel of Mark. There he found a passage that one searches in vain in the Bible editions of the churches: "The young man came to Jesus. He wore a linen robe over his bare body. And he spent the night with Jesus, who initiated him into the mysteries of the kingdom of God. "

Why did you take that out of the Bible and what else have you kept secret? Because such references could be given en masse. In principle, it would not be anything special if Jesus and his disciples were together with pleasure, but rather quite naturally. In his teaching, Jesus placed love above everything else. Why should he condemn it and not accept it with gratitude, the wonderful lustful love that he felt physically as a Son of man and that had to be a gift from God and existed all around him? Why shouldn't he initiate the young man who came to him with a robe under which he was naked and with whom he spent the night, as it was probably originally written in the Gospel of Mark?

If it was so, and there are serious supporters for it, then nothing is right at all in the Church's sex doctrine. Because then everyone would have to be equally happy about the lustful love, whether between man and woman or between the same sex. Just as evolution, which I believe comes from universal consciousness (or, as the Church says, from God) has always foreseen.

Of course, to this day in the Catholic Church, the assumed thousands of worldwide cases of sexual activities of their representatives with underage youths and the pleasurable activities of adult church members among one another and with prostitutes are kept silent or evasive. Because if you were to address it openly, you would have to honestly say why that is.

Sometimes, however, a few cases are made public. In April 2019 a case became known and the truth content was also confirmed by church representatives:

"Callboy in the Vatican unpacks: He had dozens of priests as customers - a network of gay and pedophile priests
The next sex scandal shakes the Catholic Church. Not only that so and so many priests, monks, and nuns have already been punished for child abuse and child sexual abuse, several high-ranking cardinals have already been convicted and the revelations have not stopped - now

a callboy has also written and unpacked a book. He names around 40 Catholic priests in it. Francesco Mangiacapra only made some of the customers public....

The 30-year-old homosexual callboy didn't just write the book. He also handed evidence to the Archbishop of Naples, Crescenzio Cardinal Sepe: 1200 screenshots of chat histories and very intimate photos. This dossier has since been forwarded to the Vatican. It's 1233 pages full of evidence he's accumulated over the years. Cardinal Sepe has confirmed the authenticity of this evidence to the daily newspaper "La Repubblica" and spoke of "serious cases". There should be sentences in the chats, such as ..."

Source:

Connective. Events

There is only one honest reason for this and for many other scandals: The rules and norms of sexual behavior of people, which the Church has represented for thousands of years, are so unnatural and inhuman that even church dignitaries cannot adhere to them. All these rules would have to be abolished without replacement.

But that would considerably weaken the stability of the church, at least some powerful representatives believe. But considering that this stability is built on lies and hypocrisy that has developed in them for thousands of years, then it would be right to admit and correct this mistake. In this way, they could free their priests and the overwhelming majority of their believers from "sin" and lead them to happy and fulfilling lives. Why, for God's sake, does the Catholic Church find it so difficult? To be credible, she would have to finally acknowledge that all of her prohibitions on the free sexual development of men were a grave mistake. And she should get that damn word "sin" out of your vocabulary right away. It is never a "sin" when people, regardless of gender and age, are together in lustful love. It is a "gift of God" for all, and that is how He set it up for us.

We have to recognize that the development of false norms, prejudices, and beliefs about the sexual development of human beings, which began about 3000 years ago, was not a positive development of civilization, but a short-term, fatal development that had dramatic consequences. We have to change that!

Man will always be part of evolution, which is subject to order above him, no matter what he does. Our sexual lustful feelings are also subject to it and we should be grateful for it. We have to recognize this, finally, be able to feel free again and use it for our happy and fulfilled life. We must create all the conditions for this in our society.

Sexual diversity should not, as is common today, coexist in subcultures that at most accept one another. What exists next to each other can quickly be demonized again. That is why it must finally be reintegrated on an equal footing in all groups in society. This is an important, if not the most important, aspect in the further development of the human being. It serves the expansion of our consciousness, social development, and physical evolutionary development.

5. Change prejudices and false beliefs

Before the emergence of the great religions, the sexual development of human beings was severely disturbed by the development described during the time of the division of the world, by conquests and absolutist power relations. Sex was used more or less only to satisfy her urges. There was usually a lack of the fulfilled social cohesion that sustained sexual pleasure for thousands of years. More and more people did it out of pure pleasure. That did not fill and satisfy her for long. Even in this time, there were romantic and sexually fulfilled love relationships, but they were rare, and soon the "great love" was over, if it came about at all. Unfortunately, in many historical stories and films today this is very glorified and misrepresented.

This unsatisfactory drive-controlled sex, which was no longer integrated into people's social cohesion, prepared the breeding ground for prejudices and false beliefs. At that time, the ruling class made the gradually emerging religions based on monotheism their instrument of power. The religious leaders were pushed into this role and ultimately played along to strengthen their position. As a result, the conditions for human-free, happy sexual development continued to deteriorate. The strict prohibitions and commands imposed by the church gained greater influence and settled in people's minds. In doing so, they consolidated prejudices and false beliefs, some of which are still prevalent today.

Which of the most important prejudices were shaped by religions at the time?

Sex can only take place in marriage, otherwise, it is impure. Although sex before marriage is the rule in our part of the world, there are still not a few people who feel guilty if they live out their sexual lust before marriage without restraint or who are judged for it by others.

Sex is based on lifelong loyalty to a partner. Everything else is to be condemned. Even today, cheating is mostly outlawed as unforgivable. This is massively planted in the media, but above all in films and books, very emotionally and thus effectively in people's heads.

Sex with the same sex is unnatural and dirty. Despite education and legal equality in progressive societies, this prejudice is still in the minds of many people. For too long they have had to suppress their natural, ubiquitous bisexuality. That still created a great fear of it today and ultimately led to wrong beliefs and feelings. But everything is still within us, waiting for its liberation. It takes time to get that back to normal.

Sexual thoughts of any kind outside of marriage are to be condemned. That has changed today, but even today many people more or less suppress their own, actually quite natural, lustful thoughts and sexual dreams. The repressed can not be lived out and lead to fulfillment for more happiness and satisfaction but causes dissatisfaction and frustration.

Often there is a seamless transition from prejudice to belief. However, beliefs are often directed against yourself. How you assess yourself and your situation. Beliefs are no longer pigeonholed like prejudices, but deep, emotional, general influences and convictions. To interpret the world and act on it, we need beliefs. For building a happy, sexually fulfilled life, there are helpful and hindering beliefs that are shaped by the respective social, ideological, and societal conditions. Regardless of this, you also have your sexual dreams and desires, most of which cannot be fulfilled by your current beliefs. You can incorporate these into your old beliefs or transform them into new ones.

There are two difficulties in changing wrong beliefs:

I. You have to identify your wrong beliefs first because they often affect your thinking and feeling without even being aware of it, so it is difficult to recognize them at all and to accept them as wrong. Listen to your innermost feelings and turn everything else off. Your soul is older than these teachings. She can give you the right answer in the language of feelings. The questions that follow will help.

II. Beliefs cannot be changed with your mind because of the strong manifestation. So it is not easy, because it cannot be changed sustainably through the direct path of our thinking alone, even if we have identified it as wrong. The best way to change them is to rewrite existing beliefs and feel that they are correct. So work a lot with your feelings, because they come from your soul and are right.

However, some of you may be embarrassed by the word sex. If you are one of these people, then say this word over and over again in your mind or out loud. Sex, sex; sex; ... Develop positive feelings in the process. Sex is a gift for everyone that makes them happy. Gradually feel this happiness as they keep saying the word. This is how you will free yourself from your blockages.

Then ask yourself the following questions and answer them for yourself. You are completely undisturbed when answering the questions. Nobody hears your answer. They are non-binding, also for you. Therefore, listen to your innermost feelings and be honest. Don't think about it, just let it all out. If you want, write down the answers.

Am I happy with my sex life?

Do I want a more fulfilling sex life?

Am I living out my sexual dreams and desires?

What thoughts are holding me back from living happier sexually?

How would I feel if I fulfilled my sexual dreams and desires?

Are the reasons that keep me from living a sexually fulfilling life justified?

Do I harm anyone if I live out my sexual dreams and desires?

If necessary, clear out your prejudices now.

Which beliefs keep you from fulfilling your sexual wishes and which ones help you?

To give you some support, I would like to list some general approaches to such beliefs at this point. They can of course only serve as examples and are not exhaustive. There are simply too many for that and they are dependent on each of you and what you have experienced and what you want. I will therefore give you some general approaches that can lead to inhibiting beliefs that delay or prevent the fulfillment of your sexual wishes. This will let you see how it works. Then you can then formulate very specific situations yourself.

The first belief: "Sex is not everything in life, there are more important things."

This belief already contains a great deal, sometimes no longer conscious resignation. Since you don't have such a sparkling, lustfully fulfilled life, you simply set other priorities and thus suppress your naturally lustful side. But that certainly prevents them from living happy and fulfilled. Change this belief:

Changed first belief: "Sex is not everything in life, but a full, lustful life makes me much happier and that's why I have a right to it and I want it that way."

With this belief, they claim their right to happiness and that is the most important thing in life. You know and feel exactly how happy a full, lusty life can make you.

The second belief: "If I did that, the others would never accept it or would abuse and brand me, or I would lose my family and friends, etc."

Unfortunately, it is still the case that many have prejudices and the thought "What would the others say?" Often plays a major role in realizing one's sexual desires. After all, they are usually in a socially familiar environment and do not want to be questioned in it. Remember, however, that it is not you who question those around you in the fulfillment of your sexual bliss; the others would do so. Often you just believe that others react negatively to it and then wonder why it isn't. But even if they did, should they forego their luck? Would the others do it the other way around for you? So change this belief:

Changed second belief: "I alone have the power to decide about my happiness, just like every other person I know. Nobody has the right to prescribe something or give me advice, because only I know what makes me happy and that's exactly how I want to live. "

As a rule, those around you will accept it if you confidently stand behind it. And if not, then you are most certainly not alone with your sexual desires and you will make new friends. Because an existing social environment that does not accept that you follow a path on which you will find your fulfillment is questionable from the start and not worth following. It is your life. That is why you prefer to live happily and align your social environment accordingly. The third belief: "I cannot do that because then I will hurt another."

This belief is often used when you are in a monogamous partnership. The decisive factor is how strong your bond is and how your partner feels about you. Talk to him or her. Give him/her the book to read if he/she doesn't already have it. Usually, you will find a common path to more happiness and joy or more tolerance. Just be open and honest, and if you want to keep your partner, be the same with him/her. Say and show him/her. Often the relationship for two becomes happier again. Change the belief.

Modified third belief: "I don't want to hurt anyone, but I also have the right to be happy with relish. I will always have to find a solution for this together with my partner. "

It is important to have a conversation with mutual respect and honesty. Maybe your partner has dreams and desires that you don't know about yet, and you will find a common path that suits both of you. Or maybe you will try it out first together and find a pleasurable, fulfilling path for you. Either for the two of you together or each for yourself. Even in a previously monogamous partnership, it can lead to unimagined heights. Be brave and stick to your wishes. It is your life and happiness that you decide.

The fourth belief: "I can't do that. That's not normal."

If your wishes and dreams are for a sexually fulfilled life, then it is natural and normal. You have to recognize and accept that. If you don't harm anyone in the process, you can give free rein to your lust. Nobody then has the right to judge it. Even if you're just curious about it, just test it. Experiment to your heart's content as long as it makes you happy. Sometimes you have to find your way first. Change that belief.

Modified fourth belief: "I can live out my sexual desire as I want and as often as I want. I can test myself and find my way. That is natural and completely normal. "

As long as you do not harm anyone and you do not harm yourself, the way is free for you to lead an unrestrained, lustful life. Find your fulfillment and your path in it. This will have a very positive effect on your whole happiness in life.

The fifth belief: "I can not find anyone who suits me to fulfill my sexual desires. Or nobody wants me. "

This belief is often based on disappointments one has experienced. Perhaps you are still clinging to a past relationship and comparing it to the new opportunities that are then not good enough for you. Rejections also weaken your self-esteem and you lose the courage to just keep looking. Sometimes, however, it is also unconscious prejudices that do not reveal an opportunity or you reject it from the outset, although you might have been very happy with it. Therefore, focus only on your desires and your happiness.

Changed fifth belief: everyone can find more than just one partner to be happy with relish. I will open up and for sure find the right people and then I am ready to finally do it unrestrainedly.

Based on this, you can identify and change other beliefs that are holding you back from a full and happy life.

6. Pleasure instead of frustration

Throughout the development of mankind, enjoyable togetherness was a natural and important part of life. It was freely and publicly acted out for the longest time since human existence. And the children were there all the time and saw it as something natural. From the beginning, her beliefs were shaped by a free sexual life and it led her seamlessly and with no problems into sexually mature adulthood.

What about living out our lust today?

There are many options. But are they really good and contribute to a fulfilling and happy life? Is www.fremdiegen.de a real alternative to act out our sexual urges, also outside of marriage? Or do we just live in the wrong concept of life?

Right from the beginning of human evolution, sex was no longer solely geared towards the satisfaction of pleasure but had a qualitatively new meaning. It also had an impact on people's social coexistence. The more often we live out impersonal or personal sex only to satisfy our desires, the more we move away from it. We deprive ourselves of one of the most important opportunities as social beings to lead a fulfilled and happy life.

6.1 Is marriage a pleasure killer today?

Let's first look at marriage. It arose in our present form with the religions and is still referred to as the foundation of society by politics. Marriage is "well" regulated in our society and it is still difficult for many to evade these rules. Besides, there are our own beliefs that have firmly manifested themselves in our heads over time. Marriage should last for a lifetime and usually presupposes a monogamous relationship. It was only recently softened a bit. 70 years ago it was said: "What God brought together, the man should not divide." And that was a dogma.

But marriage no longer worked the way it was supposed to. Certainly, it was not God who brought two people together in a lifelong marriage, but the Church. Especially after the sixties of the last century, when sexual education began and women gradually freed themselves from the dominant rule of men, there were unmistakable protests against this dogma. That is why divorces were then also allowed by the Catholic Church, which is now more and more carried out after a few years.

To be clear:

Of course, people in love can marry each other today. You want to show others that they love each other and feel that they belong together. I can be happy about that too. It's wonderful to celebrate the love between two people like this. It's a beautiful custom. But it should not be more than a custom and not, as it is today, still the only socially supported concept of living together. So it should not be so legally founded. So that there are no major hurdles to overcome in the event of a later change in the concept of life between the two people. But I don't generally doubt that there can be a lifelong relationship between two people. But that does not have to be stipulated by society. With recognition by society, other concepts of life should also be able to exist alongside them on an equal footing. An uncomplicated change between life concepts must be possible.

The average age at marriages increased for women and men in Germany. While it was 26.1 years for women in 1991, it was 31.5 years in 2016. In men, it rose from 28.5 to 34 years at the same time. This can also be an indication that at least young people do not want to commit so quickly. They want to live out their sexual freedom. Ultimately, however, many see marriage as the only alternative. With government support, they can live in a stable social relationship and start a family. The statistics also show us what happens afterward in many cases.

The divorce of marriages in Germany is currently around 38%. In my work I cannot compile reliable statistics myself; I have not been able to interview enough people who were married and with whom I have spoken in confidence. The few people I spoke to, without exception, confirmed to me in real life that after 4 to 8 years in marriage they no longer had sex or only very rarely. Of these, however, almost half remained monogamous, so they completely renounced a fulfilling sex life. However, 30% who had sex outside of marriage are not happy with it, 10% felt at least satisfied without being unhappy, and only 10% are completely satisfied with it. In my experience, this means that 10% of people in our country who have been married for more than eight years currently have a fulfilling sex life, but not with their partner. That doesn't exactly mean that marriage is a recipe for success for the happiness of many people.

Also, there are more and more single households that reject marriage from the outset. Especially in the big cities. In Berlin, 54.3% of households are currently single households. But also in Germany as a whole, it is 40%. 44% of them are younger than 45 years. Even if a single household does not rule out the possibility of young people being in a stable relationship, they can usually live out their sexual pleasure more freely with several partners or chance acquaintances. Turning to masturbation with the help of the telephone or the Internet, as well as films and devices, are also playing an increasingly important role.

No matter how you live as a single, in most cases, they don't build solid social ties. They are either superficial or unreliable from the start, or they resolve quickly. A sexually fulfilled pleasure does not serve to build a strong social cohesion in a group. From my experiences with clients, single life leads to more loneliness in the long run, despite an often very frequent and varied sexual life and sometimes to a quirk. It is an emergency exit from marriage, but it usually only leads to a dead end.

The development also shows that there are more and more young people, mostly young men, who simply get stuck in their families. They reject marriage and don't think much of being a single person. Which is instinctively right at first. But simply staying in the family does not bring them a happy and sexually fulfilled life in the long run. On the contrary: For many natural reasons, young and old are becoming increasingly dissatisfied in such a small space and with such close social ties. Again, a multi-generational family can be something very positive.

This development clearly shows that alternatives have to be created. In the thinking of people, in society, in the creation of new social conditions, and the resumption of sexually diverse life.

But first the questions:

So is marriage in the long run a sex killer and thus thwart a happy and fulfilling life? YES.

Can married couples do something about it? YES.

In our day and age, we are still largely driven by the institution of marriage to a monogamous life, organizationally, morally, and fundamentally. This kind of sexual development of the human being does not correspond to his nature. However, it often gets them into trouble and makes them feel unnecessarily guilty. Most people cannot achieve full sexual fulfillment in this way. This diminishes the attitude to life and narrows a fulfilled life.

With the invention of the media, starting with the printing press, there were more and more ways to lead people into monogamous lives. The first love stories emerged. The deep love was unassailable and beautiful and of course, required a lifelong loyalty. "And if they haven't died, then they are still alive today." Love stories, love dramas, and love tragedies had one thing in common: absolute loyalty or the demonization of unfaithfulness. They still enchant people today and that already begins in childhood. So if you hear and read about these stories from all sides over and over again, then it arouses needs, even if they are unrealistic or do not correspond to your nature.

The advertising specialists know about it. They are especially effective when they are emotionally bound. This is how permanent monogamous marriage is made palatable to them. It is brainwashing on a global scale, and most people participate unconsciously. However, this leads to despair and frustration at the latest when, after a few attempts, you have to realize that you are unable to build such a long-lasting, beautiful relationship in real life. Many then look for the fault within themselves. This is wrong! Another possibility, perhaps just as good or better, is not shown to them. So they are disappointed with life.

That is tragic because life can be much more beautiful than it is described in these films or books. You just have to know and find out about it. But since it is the marriage that the prevailing ideology wants, they will not be shown the loving, fulfilling, and happy life in a group. If they had heard of such stories always and everywhere from childhood and not of the monogamous, mostly exclusively heterosexual love relationships, they would today also have a different attitude and different wishes and, according to their nature, would be able to lead a happy and sexually fulfilled life.

Since love and sex in a couple of relationships always form an inseparable unit in these stories, one also believes that it is an unforgivable breach of trust if the partner had sex with someone else. We are constantly showered with such an ideology from childhood. It shapes beliefs and creates twisted ideals, which then leads to heartache, jealousy, and a thousandfold tragedy. That is why so many beautiful connections have often broken up painfully. But love is always selfless and must not be demanding or possessive. This is exactly what they do when they demand loyalty during sex. People can also fall in love with multiple people. Love is the basic feeling of creation and does not always refer to one person, not even in terms of sexual fulfillment. And so they have lived happily in groups or extended families for hundreds of thousands of years. That was their nature and was very beneficial for their development and would still be today.

Loyalty can be very nice when you are in love, but in the vast majority of cases, it is not permanent. At most, one can force oneself to be faithful or be morally forced to do so, but that does not make one happy. Deep down, everyone feels that when they are not freshly in love. And when two people are freshly in love, then they should also live monogamous for as long as both want, but without clinging or having claims to the other. But the proclaimed "eternal love" and loyalty between two people from many quarters, especially by the media, makes many believe that it just has to be that way, creating jealousy and painful lovesickness. Feelings that never existed before and that cost many people their lives every year.

Of course, people can also love each other forever. Even in a polygamous or bisexual relationship, the relationship between two people can remain strong and happy, but it doesn't have to be. For example, sexual freedom should not be granted to a partner on the condition that he or she stays with him. You can't give someone something that you don't have at all. Everyone is free in their sexual and social development. The only social bond and responsibility a person has are the children they have or have children. And that can be designed very differently for the benefit of all.

But here, too, people were particularly wrongly influenced by the media. In many films, dramas are shown where children suffer because mom and dad split up.

For one thing, you will only get ideologically sprinkled once again, because in the real world this is usually not the case, and good opportunities are found that children do not suffer from. If there are problems with it, it is often not the divorce itself, but the manner and foreplay that lead to it. And that is again due to our prejudices and beliefs that we embody with our behavior. On the other hand, it only shows clearly that marriage as a principle of life also proves to be unsuitable in this relationship. For example, if children live in a larger group or extended family from the outset, such problems will not arise.

6.2. Alternative life concepts

Above all, the hippie movement in the sixties of the last century showed us how. They lived out the feeling of peace and free love. They loved each other and lived out their sexual lust together, regardless of gender. The only thing that counted was the love and bliss in the sexual ecstasy that they experienced as a couple or as a group of the opposite or same-sex. This concept was finally back to human nature and they felt free from the constraints and guilt feelings that were otherwise common in the Christian society from which they came.

But they were also pioneers in raising children in an anti-authoritarian manner, without violence and beatings. The children grew up in a larger social group and were accompanied by them together until adulthood. Children need to discover and understand their world to ultimately find their place in it. Even lustful tenderness was something quite natural for them that was not hidden from them. In her group, it was lived out freely in front of her eyes. You have to keep in mind that at that time outside of the community even kissing in public was forbidden. As children, they could pursue and explore their feelings of pleasure according to their needs and will. So they grew into a sexually happy life that they could freely develop without any problems.

They had a lot of questions. In a group, they have the opportunity to understand their world better because they had several contacts. They also experienced conflict resolution in the community and were not excluded from it. That created trust. They learned in the process and addressed their problems and conflicts openly and on an equal footing with their elders. In such a group they also had much more diverse orientation options to develop their dispositions, skills, and talents. And through the anti-authoritarian upbringing, they had the freedom to test it out. They were able to try out things that interested them, gain more personal experience, and were not pressured to do anything. Many prejudices were not even implanted in them because they were not manipulated by the media, because there was no television, cinema, or news.

Through this anti-authoritarian upbringing of children, this movement significantly supported the then introduced ban on beatings in school and violence in the family. Because beforehand, in many countries around the world, parents were allowed to beat their children as they saw fit and teachers to beat their students. The pedagogical teachings then changed, as far as the conditions at that time in a society in which the monogamous marriage, with its outdated, sometimes mendacious morals, prevailed.

The hippies at that time a completely new concept and mistakes were made too. Experience would have required them the time to learn, and they should have had the chance to create optimal conditions for it. But they didn't get it. On the contrary, they were branded as dropouts from society from the start. They were put under increasing pressure and fought wherever possible. It did not correspond to the prevailing ideology. So ultimately this attempt to create better social relationships for a happier and more fulfilling life failed. The prerequisites for this were much worse than they are today.

Nevertheless, they gave people a lasting attitude towards life that most secretly longed for. Their wonderful music, which was celebrated worldwide, carried this attitude towards life into people's hearts. Especially with the youth. It was the start of the so-called sexual revolution. Sex has been talked about publicly again for a long time. People talked about their problems and desires. They wanted to be freer and be able to live out their wishes. The norms shifted and they gained some freedom. This turned out to be particularly positive for the women who were previously more or less without rights, also in the area of their sexual fulfillment.

However, I do not want to speak of a "revolution", because the old basic rules of lifelong marriage, heterosexuality, and monogamy were essentially retained, even if they were softened. No thought was given to a new form of living together for the full development of love and sexual fulfillment. Most people were still caught up in their old prejudices and beliefs.

The children continued to be excluded from sex and the conflicts that arose in a monogamous marriage, despite realizing it. For them, the firm belief was so shaped that one does not talk about it. So they didn't do the same to their parents when they came of age themselves. Later offers to her: "You can talk to me about anything" This no longer helped. And that's still the case today.

So what are the alternatives today if you are currently living in an unfulfilled marriage?

On average, every adult person aged 20 to 50 thinks about sex 15 times a day. There are no major differences between the sexes, as the latest studies have shown. You can get sex anywhere today. Thanks to the internet. Psychologically or physically, spontaneous, anonymous sex is very attractive, but since it is always associated with feelings that cannot develop in this way, it remains unsatisfactory in the long run. This is also the case with frequently changing sex and ultimately leads to frustration and loneliness.

Even in a marriage, people have a sense of togetherness. This is so important to him that he often later renounces a sexually fulfilled life and stays with his trusted partner. But humans are not monogamous by nature and have long-term pleasurable desires that they want to satisfy. And that is exactly the problem in a monogamous marriage for two and leads to dissatisfaction and arguments. I know a lot of marriages where the partners constantly attack and argue, but still don't break up because they're afraid of being alone. They then imagine that they are still attached to their partner, although he mostly only annoys them. But what kind of life is that? I have more than enough case studies from my practical work. But they're just sad and uninteresting. That's why I don't want to describe them here.

So in this respect too, marriage, as it exists today, is not a solution. Yeah, it's not even just out of date. But from the beginning, it was the wrong way to a happy life. It arose out of necessity. Later the people were forced to do so by the Church. We cannot simply change the beliefs that have developed from this in all people overnight. Added to this are the social conditions that marriage still sees and promotes as the most important form of coexistence. That certainly does not allow rapid change. We need new ways of life that are also borne and supported by society, like marriage today. So what are the alternatives at the moment? From evolution and personal experiences in the conversations, however, a sexually fulfilled life must always be seen in the context of the social aspect. Anonymous or faster socially independent sex is not the way to go. But you could, for example, make your sex life more open in marriage and look for the right partner for it. But do it freely and openly with one another. Do not use it to marginalize your partner. That usually leads to problems.

Unfortunately, under the current conditions, you will hardly find any couples or individuals from your immediate social circle, although that would be the best way to go. But you can look for a swingers club, for example. Middle-aged couples in their fifties also visit and have fun there. Swinger clubs even exist for bisexual couples. Go there and meet like-minded people who you will then meet there more often. This has the advantage that you don't have to let strangers into your private area to get to know them. Ideally, build up a friendly and social relationship first and only live out your lustful side after the third or fourth meeting.

Epilogue

In the vast majority of cases, monogamous, lifelong marriage does not lead to a sexually fulfilled and permanently happy life. I don't know of a single case. It can only be improved somewhat if the couples live together tolerantly. To achieve free sexual development again, new forms of coexistence are also required. One form would be living in groups or "extended families" with several men and women.

In addition to sexual development, this can have many other advantages:

Everyone could freely live out their polygamous and bisexual side. But everyone should be able to do it completely freely according to their feelings and wishes. There should also be room for a monogamous two-way relationship that is unlimited in time. Anyone who has ever been in love also knows that it can be a wonderful time.

A group life would not only lead to free sexual development but would gradually replace the anonymous sex outside of marriage that is prevalent today.

The space for claiming ownership or jealousy would be very small. Ideally, it wouldn't even exist. This mostly works well in bisexual relationships in a group.

A group always consists of several people who can complement and support each other better and in more diverse ways.

In a group, everyone retains their individuality, as nobody has to adjust to living together with just one person. As an individual personality with his abilities, talents, and interests he can contribute to the whole group and usually find more recognition in it. This strengthens self-confidence and satisfaction.

The division of labor in the group can be better based on interests and skills. In this way, the work will be more fun and more successful there, which everyone will benefit from.

Children in the group have everyone as contact persons. This is a huge benefit for their development. Your many questions will be answered faster and better and you can look for role models more often in the group. Any negative, uncontrolled external influences are lower. They become more confident and talk more openly about their feelings and problems. In this way, they can grow into adulthood much more easily and develop optimally.

Children grow up in a group that leads a sexually free life. They too will freely develop their lust and grow naturally into a sexually mature age without blockages and secrecy.

A group develops a group dynamic for itself and the children who grow up in it, which has a positive effect on everyone.

Surely some will now say: "It all happened before and it failed." It happened in the seventies and eighties of the last century. These movements started with the youth. During this time there have never been so many young people concerning the proportion of the population. They came from the post-war baby boom. It was a generation that knew no war and was able to deal with its wishes and needs like no other before. They didn't want to adopt the old, dusty norms of their parents. They wanted to live differently.

This resulted in communities that also lived more sexually. The motive was mostly to protest against the existing order. There was no inner drive to want to do better and thus to develop and grow this way of life. On the other hand, there was still massive resistance from many directions in society at this time. It was a brave start, but there were many other important issues at the time that had to be pushed through through massive protest and pressure: like the introduction of the pill, abortion, the repeal of the law banning homosexuality, and much more. So this concept of life failed at that time. But was that wrong?

Today, these or other social life concepts can arise because the conditions are much better. They can arise from the knowledge that the existing forms of coexistence do not work for most of them or do not lead to further development and a fulfilled life. It is not just different concepts, but better ones that can be developed today. It does not have to be just this group that I have suggested. Although I think it's good at the moment.

I once had a discussion in a group about whether two men and one woman or two women and one man or two men and two women and so on could "marry" to start an extended family together. That with one man and several women still exists today and in a few areas also with one woman and several men.

In these ideas, the legal obligation and probably also the protection for such a family were important. That, too, would of course be an alternative if the gender distribution and their sexual orientation could be freely decided. Maybe other members can join later if necessary and desired. This would have the advantage that already existing marriages could modify their contract with more than one.

The decisive factor in everything is how far and quickly we free ourselves from our prejudices and fixed beliefs and how quickly society reacts to them and creates the conditions for them. With everything that evolution has taught us so far, it would be an enormous step forward in the development of human life in that it can uncover unimagined potential.

7. The children's feelings of pleasure

To be clear right from the start: It's about pleasurable feelings, not sexual ones because children don't have them. Children have not been excluded from the feelings of sexual pleasure of adult members of a community for hundreds of thousands of years. Most of the time they were there and watched the joyful ecstatic get-together. They then playfully explored what they had seen in their innocence among one another and asked questions. For her, none of this was anything special and was part of life. Everything was gladly explained and shown to them so that they could take full advantage of this wonderful opportunity at a sexually mature age. Children also feel lustful feelings that they could live out naturally in their group. In this way, they grew happily and freely into adulthood.

Certainly, cultural differences also have to be considered here.

The idea of pedophilia as we know it today is also a result of the prohibitions that emerged only two thousand years ago. The natural development process of the children was thereby considerably restricted. That had consequences for her and the adult. To comply with the new rules, the children were forbidden to enjoy activities and were defined as wrong and bad.

In my view, they have been abused by depriving them of the natural development of their sensations of pleasure. Over time, this led to false beliefs. They then passed on these beliefs from generation to generation and they became stronger and stronger. Showing lustful affection was only allowed for adults. The natural pleasurable childish feelings were considered bad. Since then it has also been reprehensible for adults to share these non-sexual caresses with children. It was forbidden and severely punished. This deprivation of tenderness made the children anxious and insecure when they reached sexual maturity. They lacked the natural seamless transition of their sexual development.

This new, nature-contradicting way of dealing with pleasurable feelings generated tension and disorientation, which then led to undesirable developments. This is how pedophilia, as we know it today, came about.

Children are sexually seduced and forced into secrecy or blackmailed. Since they have lustful feelings about it, they are persuaded to be guilty. That harms them emotionally. Today, however, they are often physically abused against their will. A real business with child sex emerged. Child pornography and prostitution are only part of it. The real cause of this development, however, goes back 2000 years. Despite all these undesirable developments, children are full of love and also full of lustful feelings that make them very happy. Don't be afraid of them, give them that affection. Give your children the physical contact and the caresses. Also allow your children to give their children their devoted and lustful hugs as often as they want. It can never be too much. This is something very beautiful and has absolutely nothing to do with pedophilia.

A young man came to talk to me about this. He was 25 years old. He told me that he had a nephew with whom he had a very warm relationship. This boy was eleven years old. Once he had clung to him again. He wanted to cuddle and be petted. The young man did that too, as so often. Over time, he noticed that something was moving in the boy. It was his penis that got stiff. Now he didn't know what to do anymore, because the boy had pressed even closer to him. So he stroked his back and whispered: "It's all good." He wanted to calm him down. But that made his nephew all the more let out his lustful feelings, and he got his first orgasm. His uncle quickly told him to put on another pair of trousers because they had a big stain. Then he spoke to him that he was now physically sexually mature and that he has to be a little more careful so that this doesn't happen again.

However, he was very confused now, he told me. Should he have acted differently so that that didn't happen in the first place? And how should he behave in the future? Should he tell his sister?

I looked at him beaming and said kindly, "I congratulate you. She was lucky enough to see her nephew become a man. "He looked at me confused. Then I continued: "You did nothing wrong. You didn't want it and your nephew was surely also very surprised. The first orgasm can be uncontrollable and sudden. Only, in the end, you could have shown him more joy about this important and beautiful event. Tell your sister exactly as it happened and then celebrate with your nephew and sister a little celebration of his sexual maturity. Make him feel that something beautiful and great is waiting for him from now on and that you will be happy with him. Make him proud of it. "

Even before your children reach sexual maturity, they will ask you many questions about it. Talk to them openly and honestly about it. You will also playfully explore this side of yourself with other children and you should give them this freedom and support them. Let it happen and enjoy your child's curiosity, just as you do on other occasions. When it happens or did happen, speak to them with full understanding. It's a natural process. In this way, they become self-confident and happy people, with an unencumbered development of their sexual desire their life will become more beautiful and fulfilling.

A client came to me and said in a relaxed manner:

"I have a nine-year-old daughter. She is very lively and very good at school. Now I came into her room a few days ago and she was lying on the bed. Two boys from their class sat to the right and left. She had no panties on and one boy had his hand on her pussy and played with it while the other watched. I was shocked, but remained calm and asked, "What are you doing?" The boys stopped immediately. But my daughter replied, "Mom, it's nice when he plays with it." I asked her to put the panties back on and I told the boys to go.

At the moment I didn't know what to say, I ran out of the room to calm down again. A little later I asked her if she had done this before. She told me that so far she has only done it with Maik, her best friend from school. But today he brought his friend with him, who had never seen anything like it. He should take a look at it too. Then I told her not to do that anymore. She asked me: "Why not?" "Because you don't do that," I replied. After that she was calm. However, I noticed that she was not satisfied with this answer and I am afraid she will continue to do so. What can I do against it?"

I explained to her that it was completely normal and natural for children to playfully explore their sexuality and, above all, their differences. They too already have feelings of pleasure and are curious about it. This also includes touching and being touched. That can also give them a lot of pleasure among themselves. So for now it's nothing to worry about. Explain to your daughter that she has curiosity and lust, which is very beautiful, and that this lust becomes even more beautiful when she is sexually mature. She can look forward to that. You understand that she is curious about it.

But tell her that these experiences with lust are something very personal and intimate. You only share these wonderful feelings with people you like. So she shouldn't do it with someone just because someone is curious about it or because she just likes it. So she should tell Maik that he shouldn't bring any more friends because of that. That would be too superficial for this beautiful thing. She'll understand that. Do not make dramatic or moral comments or prohibitions. She won't understand. So when she's studying or playing alone with her best friend in the room again, don't keep looking in to see what they're doing. "

Suppressed and often misunderstood feelings of pleasure in childhood sometimes spill over into adulthood, later lead to misinterpretation and mental disorders, sometimes to pedophilia.
Another client came to me and said:
"I have a friend who has a seven-year-old girl. This little one is very affectionate and always wants to cuddle. Sometimes she does it so passionately that it excites me a lot. I've also casually touched her intimate caressing once and she seemed to like it. "He asked me how far he could go. Even this question made me wonder. So I asked him if he had often felt this excitement in children, and he confirmed it to me. He replied that he thought of little girls very often, and sometimes of boys too. Even as a child he liked to play doctor games with both sexes. When he reached sexual maturity, he had contact with a nine-year-old boy who visited him sometimes and liked to satisfy him with his hand and mouth. And although the boy wanted it himself, he was insulted and punished when his mother caught him doing it. After that, he didn't do it anymore. But the memory of it excited him further and he developed more

and more fantasies. "I felt that the boy liked it a lot too. Then he always came to me by himself. "

Now I said to him, "If you are a pedophile, you shouldn't take it down on it, even if you and the childlike it at first. Children can also feel pleasure and are curious about it, which is quite normal. The boy felt the joy it gives you and he liked it, but he did not have these strong feelings. Of course, he found it interesting and beautiful and you had just discovered this sexual pleasure in you and found it very beautiful too. You shouldn't have been scolded and punished for this, but now you are in a different situation. Maybe you say to yourself: It doesn't have to be more than warm hugs and caresses. But it won't stay that way because you are a grown man now and have strong secondary fantasies. Your sexual desire will make you go on and on. Just think about how your fantasies about this child have already developed. You will no longer be able to register whether the child still likes it or not. Even if the child doesn't protest, your actions will overwhelm them. Later, especially because of the social assessment, they will reproach themselves and get big problems in their social behavior. From my work with young people, I do not know of a case where it was not the case. So if you love the child, you can't do that to her. If you do it anyway, then it's selfish pleasure gratification. In doing so, they accept that they may cause emotional harm to the child. And that is a criminal offense, even if you are only a victim of historical development. If you cannot do this on your own, you have to get help and separate from your friend so that you no longer have contact with the girl. "

Children feel lustful when they are hugged and caressed. The older they get, the stronger they are. That is completely natural and beautiful. Parents have often asked me where the limits are: What can and cannot be allowed? I answered it like this:

As a rule, it is not the physical limits that need to be observed. The limit begins where sexual arousal arises in the adult and the thought of further sexual acts takes hold. The child should not be forbidden to do so. Only when you notice that it is getting stronger and stronger, you shouldn't necessarily incite it with more intense pats. But don't stop completely because of that, because then it will probably be ashamed of it and under no circumstances should it. So don't show sudden reluctance or even rejection. Not even if you notice that you are easily aroused by it. It's a natural reaction. As an adult, however, you can usually deal with it without it leading to sexual activity. But if it becomes too much for you, then slowly and carefully end this tenderness in this situation with loving-kindness. If this happens more often and you then find it uncomfortable, find out where and when your child reacts particularly pleasurably. Distract them from it or avoid them without them noticing. However, if your child does not stop doing it, then tell them kindly that you do not like it. In this situation, the children themselves learn to say "no" if they feel the same way.

The desire of the children does not pursue the goal of sexual satisfaction and they are overwhelmed when another does it. It cannot, therefore, be compared with adult sexuality. If you understand that, then you can handle it well too.

Your child has so many wonderful qualities that you will enjoy. But many of them only have children. One of them is her lustful and completely innocent devotion. Enjoy it and show it. It would be wrong to exclude this wonderful side of your child. But if you do that, it will feel it, not understand it and misinterpret it. That will stay in his mind forever. Later, your child will never fully trust you in this area. It will make a secret of it and, at worst, make it feel unlovable. I know some adults, especially women, who then had big problems in their relationships because they couldn't get rid of that feeling of not being loved, which they felt as a child, even as adults, and suffered greatly from it.

108

Epilogue

Children have probably been involved in various sexual acts at all times and in many cultures, especially since they also have lustful feelings, and sometimes even in their innocence were the initiators out of curiosity. But they never strive for sexual satisfaction.

From experience reports by clients in my practice, there were no subsequent psychological problems involuntary, intimate contacts with sexually mature adolescents and adults, which they wanted as children, as long as they were not forced to do more than they wanted. On the contrary, it was an exciting, pleasurable experience for her. Problems only arose when outside adults interfered and made something bad out of it.

It was a different matter if they had not taken the initiative of their own accord, but were seduced into it. Even if they still had lustful feelings, in the beginning, it slowly became too much for them, but it didn't stop. Then they felt overwhelmed and found it uncomfortable. If it happened to someone to whom they felt strongly emotionally attached, they did participate, sometimes again and again, but it harmed their natural sense of pleasure and thus also their later sexual development. Most of the time this did not come to light until many years later. I got to know several women and men with serious sexual and social problems.

Even greater damage occurs when they experience this with strangers or with people who have little social ties to them. At most, only initial curiosity and not lustful devotion played a role. But sometimes it is just brute force that can also occur within the family. Often you notice that in the child, at least that something is wrong with him. Most often, children are also abused in a physically painful manner in this case. This is then a traumatic experience that has to be treated professionally by a suitable psychologist.

Sexual abuse can wreak havoc, and families and society must protect children from it. Ultimately, if the child is being violated, there must be laws about it. Regardless of whether it was the violence of a sexual, physical, or emotional nature. However, one should distinguish whether it is abuse or whether it was just a pleasurable natural discovery with an older young person. What is exciting and beautiful for a child, even if it could be sexual, is often viewed differently by outside adults. If you take away these opportunities from your child and turn a harmless and enjoyable journey of discovery into a public problem in which you involve others and ask the police about it, then this can have noticeably negative long-term consequences.

I also know a few cases of this. Often it is then feelings of guilt because the young man or woman later knows that they wanted it and it was nice, but then suddenly it should be bad. Even if they weren't blamed and they were treated as victims, they still felt guilty, actually even guiltier, because someone was unjustly punished for it. They couldn't deal with that and years later they came to therapy full of doubts and feelings of guilt. You shouldn't do anything like this to your child either. Sometimes your impressions are not what your child feels about them. Pay more attention to how it came about and what your child thinks and feels about it.

Conversely, children of course still have a lot of imagination and talk about it, which can also be sexual. Often adults don't trust them with so much imagination and think it must be true. Check the truth of the matter first before you set something in motion. If you don't do it and the child's harmless fantasy turns into a lie out of fear, this can also have a very negative effect on the development of your child.

In particular, even sexually mature adolescents with false claims may want to get more attention and care from their parents or pursue other goals. Always question it when something like this is said. At this age, the children usually already know everything and maybe more than you do. I have noticed this more than once in group discussions with this age group. If you believe a lie and investigate it, it can also have devastating consequences for your child's future sexual development. And you are ruining the whole life of the innocent adult concerned. Here, too, I know cases from my practical work.

Conclusion:

Pay closer attention to how your child behaves. The first impression as an adult about a situation you encounter does not always match your child's experience. Pay attention to what your child is feeling and use that as a measure of your behavior and actions.

Enjoy your child's feelings of pleasure and don't shy away from them. Continue to be tender and loving to him.

Children's games to discover your feelings and sexuality are very natural and this is how you should treat them if you observe them. Talk to your child about it normally if they want to.

Don't hide your caresses with your partner from your child. Don't feel caught out if it suddenly comes in while you are exchanging endearments. It notices this immediately and receives the wrong signals.

8. The sexual repression of sexually mature adolescents

Even more dramatic is what sexual restriction meant for adolescents' adolescent development. If they were previously accepted into the circle of adults as full members when they reached sexual maturity, they are now still regarded as children. A legal age has been set at which they will be taken seriously as sexual beings. Before that, it is forbidden for themselves and others to perform pleasurable actions. For everyone, this is a major turning point that we can hardly understand. It is against all laws of nature. This dramatically suppresses the adolescents' wonderful sexual development. That had consequences.

8.1 The relationship between adolescents and parents during their sexual development

Adolescents in particular have great problems living out their sexual lust. They are educated in schools, but they are excluded from sexual life. Although they are sexually mature at the age of 11 to 13, they continue to be treated as children. Currently, by law, only perceived as equal sexual beings at the age of 16. In the most beautiful time of their life, which lies in the discovery and development of their sexual pleasure, they usually only do it in secret and are often reprimanded or punished if they are caught in their curious and exciting self-discovery.

This creates frustration and despair. It is no wonder that this leads to rejection of the so-called adults, aggressiveness, profuse alcohol, and drug consumption. A thorough rethinking process is urgently needed here. Our ancestors showed us and the religions carried us away from this correct and natural process, with dramatic consequences, also in the happy development of our growing child.

Therefore: After you have duly celebrated the sexual maturity of your child, talk to him or her about the many possibilities to experience these wonderful feelings. Explain to him the pleasurable parts of your now-adult body and do not hide anything. Do this with boys who had their first seminal discharge and girls who had their first period. Make them proud of it. At this point, take your child into the family of adults, no matter what the law says. From now on it has a greater say and more free decisions, but also more responsibility and tasks. Because at this point it is the right time, as it has always been. Your child will grow into a self-confident, happy person and from this point on will also take more responsibility for their actions.

When explaining sexual pleasure, do not commit yourself to one gender. So don't tell a boy, "If you have a girlfriend ..." or a girl, "If you have a boyfriend ..." when asked, tell your child that they can try out what they want for themselves. This will take away all unfounded fears from him. If you find it difficult to speak openly with your child, give them books that discuss sexual love between men and women and same-sex sexuality. If he wants to talk about it afterward, talk to him about it. Let him/her decide what to try.

If you treat your child in this way, they will find a partner more quickly with whom they can experience this. In this way, they will want to get to know their sexuality without fear and freedom and live it out full of joy. This has a positive effect on his sex life and he has the chance to lead a fulfilled and happy life with it. In this day and age, however, it is necessary to point out contraception and the health risks.

But do not do it threateningly and do not scare them with it, but explain to your child how to avoid these risks. Help him positively do this too. For example, you could go shopping for condoms with a boy. After that, take him to a place he likes. For example to McDonald's or the cinema. Make it a special and beautiful day with him.

Make sure that your child's first experiences are best within their trusted social circle of friends. Age and gender do not play a role, it is only important that there is already a familiar, emotionally positive connection in this group. You can tell whether your child is happy with it. If so, show that you are happy about it. In no case do you hold back when asked about your own sexual experiences? But wait until you are asked about it.

The affection of adults for adolescents is called Hebephilia. That, too, is still a criminal offense in our society. I think these laws are out of date. The protection against sexual harassment, coercion, and rape, which applies to everyone, is sufficient in my opinion. Everyone should be able to be with everyone with pleasure if both want it. In my opinion and experience with clients, the age or the age difference does not play a role. Reports from history have always shown that young, sexually mature people have enjoyed learning from older people. It was a very instructive and pleasurable time for both of them, not only from a sexual point of view.

There were and are clans in some regions where young sex mature women are trained by older women in physical love and female orgasm. There were and are also tribes where the medicine man shows young men how they can achieve a particularly strong orgasmic ecstasy and strengthen their virility. But also schools between men and women, by young and older partners, are often to be found in history. These reports stretch almost completely into modern times and there are certainly only a few that have been discovered. Learning from the elderly has been a tradition for over a million years, of course, also when it comes to sexuality. Every sexually mature young person should therefore be able to decide for himself. Just leave it to your child and see if they're happy with it.

Some may argue that the youngster has no experience at a young age and can therefore be easily seduced. But at this age, your child will continue to stay with their usual circle of friends and acquaintances. And if you talk to him about anything like an awakening man, then the chances are that he will be seduced by a stranger against his interest. But what I mean by that is that you talk to each other openly and don't just warn of dangers. It does not affect. "I always warned him or her about it" I've heard many times from parents who tried to do it this way, and it didn't work.

If you meet your child as I have described them at puberty, they will be confident enough and not get involved in anything questionable. At most, it can be that he didn't like what it tested afterward. But we have all already had this experience and hopefully learned from it.

Let your child grow up and only help when you notice that they cannot go on on their own. In most cases, this will be told to you by a self-confident young person with whom you have always spoken openly and honestly about this topic and who has trusted you since childhood.

In this context, I had an amusing experience.

I went to a holiday camp for a few days with some boys from socially disadvantaged families who had learning and behavioral problems. They were between 14 and 18 years old. In such an environment I could work with them very well. We lived together in a large bungalow. One day I went to our bathroom and saw a boy who was busy with his erect penis. I said quickly, but in a friendly manner: "Sorry, but you have to lock up if you want to be here alone" and wanted to go out again. He turned to me, stood in the middle of the room with his erection, and asked me if I didn't know something he could do to make him bigger. I went to him, stood up and looked down at him carefully, and said: "It's pretty big already." To which he replied: "But the girls want a bigger one". They must have looked at some pictures of grown men and raved about the large limbs about them. Now the boy was a little disappointed in his own. I looked him in the eye and said, "Hey, it's very big for your age. It will still grow by itself until you are 25 years old. It will be a powerful device one day. "He beamed at me immediately and said, relieved:" Well, then its good."

Then I ran again and as I walked I said: "Carry on, but lock the door first."

I had many open conversations with this boy afterward. He came to me on his own and spoke, among other things, about his sexual desires, dreams, and needs. We talked about everything. So I was able to give him a lot of tips and advice. Through the conversations with him, which of course he promptly told the others, questions came from other guys in group discussions on this topic. I had explained to them credibly that it was something completely natural and normal. In this way, they gained the trust and sought a conversation with me. You noticed how happy they were to finally be able to talk to an adult about it, which they sometimes confirmed to me.

It was found that in this group almost all had pleasurable experiences with older people before they reached sexual maturity, mostly with other boys but also with girls. Their experiences ranged from watching masturbation, rubbing against each other, touching, and up to the oral activity. Everyone found it exciting and interesting. When I asked if they had also spoken to their parents about it, they were very astonished. Of course, they didn't. That would mean a lot of trouble.

A boy was caught by his mother with an older boy when he was curiously about to discover new things. He was immediately forbidden to interact with him. There was no open conversation with his mother about it. He felt guilty. The mother also spoke to the parents of the other sexually mature boy who was punished. So a completely natural, pleasurable, and interesting gimmick had turned into a drama for both boys, which of course had a negative influence on their attitudes in the future.

The reason most teenagers don't talk to their parents about it today is that it's never really openly and honestly talked about from childhood. The impersonal explanations at school or an educational book from the parents do not help at all. It doesn't explain how beautiful love can be and how it enriches our lives. But if you show your child at an early age that sex is something beautiful and, above all, something completely natural that you don't have to be ashamed of, then he or she is not afraid to talk about it. Just keep talking without making them feel like you want to hear them out.

8.2. Free sexual development lies in the strength of youth

Young people between the ages of 16 and 17 have the highest sexual pleasure energy in their life. And even before that, it is already strong. Their free development is prevented or at least suppressed by social rules. This creates a lot of pressure on young, sexually mature people. There are more and more young people who between the ages of 14 and 16 have all kinds of mental problems. This ranges from poor concentration to performance failure and depression.

In my experience, sexual oppression plays a major role in this. In any case, I don't know any young people who have such problems if they already had a sex life with one or more partners at the time. Unless they feel guilty, such as "I don't want to get gay" after a boy has had fun with a friend one or more times. That's what I hear most from boys. But there are many other reasons for feeling guilty as well. And that's just because human nature is simply not recognized and lived. This is based on false norms that, despite being informed, are still firmly entrenched in the minds of most people.

I have also met many mothers who were desperate because their son or daughter suddenly had such big problems at school. That goes as far as school refusal, they told me. They always think that their child is simply overwhelmed. They did not see that it is no longer a child, but a 15 to 16-year-old man or a young woman who has great problems with the parents and teachers not recognizing their adulthood. Also because they could not let their natural wonderful sexual powers out, they often suffer. But also through their upbringing in childhood, they can have great inhibitions and struggle with internal conflicts.

This leads to the fact that more and more young people have sexual and social problems later on because at the age of the peak of their sexual pleasure they could not live them out and sometimes had to suppress them strongly. Her further pleasurable and happy social development was severely disturbed.

The right to sexual self-determination should begin with sexual maturity and not only at the age of 16. The word "minor" is also nonsense, which should be deleted in this context. Young people are raised to be "minors" at most but are not naturally so. That contradicts all-natural logic. Of course, a society must have rules that organize the coexistence of many people. But these rules should never go against nature or evolution, they should support them. And a sexually mature person is an adult. Only in this way can people develop freely and happily in it.

How can that change? Examples:

Of course, young people can live out their desires. But that should mainly happen in their familiar social environment. I can remember my school days when there were also groups within the school class who met regularly to be together with each other in a pleasurable way. Sometimes things got down to business. They were 14 or 15 years old, curious, eager to experiment, and wanted to know everything about it. At these meetings, they explored their desires. They tried the condoms there in the practice and most of the girls were already taking birth control pills. Of course, all of this took place in secret and without the parents' knowledge. You would have been the last to be discussed about it. And that's still the case today.

At this point I am addressing young people directly:

But caution is advised when strangers and older people come into play. That can go well and also be very pleasurable, but the ignorance and sexual lack of control as a young person can then be exploited. This is usually noticeable quickly, especially if young people have already confidently dealt with their sexuality in the family and know their limits. People who want to take advantage of others like to give directions on what to do. Your wishes will not be dealt with or only superficially. Perhaps you are given alcohol as a special privilege of adulthood to drink. It becomes particularly dangerous when you are asked to do the same with others. Even if there are great reasons for it. Nobody should ask that of you or try to persuade you to do so. You definitely shouldn't go into it at this age. Always choose your partner yourself and don't let anyone influence you or put you under pressure.

If you notice this, break up with such a sex partner as soon as possible, even if it is sometimes difficult. If you can't do it on your own, get help! This separation is not a problem in your development. Don't make a drama out of it for you and your emotional world. You are sure to find much better partners. Just see it as an educational experience and stop thinking about it when it's over. No matter how far you've gone such experiences are made by people of all ages, and not just young people, for a variety of reasons. I know that from my work.

Don't let your path stop you. So do not withdraw because of such an experience and therefore do not deny yourself the most beautiful thing in the world. Nobody is worth it. Just tick off those idiots. Curious and eager to experiment, find your happy path. Always be friendly and respectful to your partners. Just like you expect from him. Good, fulfilling sex is always about affection and trust. That has to build up first. Take the time you need to do it.

This is the only way you can fully open yourself to your desires and find deep fulfillment and not just hot sex and satisfaction in it. At your age, however, spontaneous sex is sometimes exciting.

I too am still thinking of a unique but wonderful experience that I had spontaneously when I was 16 on a hike through the Harz Mountains, which I will probably never forget. Just make your own experiences. You will find the way.

Young people can also, for example, set up a shared apartment. It's on the rise anyway. But it shouldn't be possible until the age of 18. Find the right partners for it. Don't just live, live with them. This usually also includes a pleasurable togetherness.

Ideally, you should also live out your bisexual side when you feel it in you or are just curious. This creates a greater sense of togetherness, is even more exciting, and leaves little room for arguments and jealousy. Everyone is loved in this group because of their uniqueness. This creates a zest for life and a healthy level of self-confidence. Experience your lust whenever and as often as you want in this free love. You will always find partners for it. It's very exciting and full of happy moments. So you will hardly get into an uncomfortable situation with strangers.

Concrete proposal

How about if, for example, there were shared apartments with people between the ages of 14 and 25, where sexual pleasure can also be fully lived out? That would be enormously beneficial for the social and sexual development of young people. This is only one example because I do not want to set any age limits downwards or upwards, neither for a young adult nor for the flatshare members. That would be another new wrong rule. It is only important that everyone feels good about it and that they are not ideologically or organizationally tied to the group. So everything happens at any time through free will and can also be ended if necessary. The possibility of changing a flatshare or returning to the family at a young age must be guaranteed. Let nature and evolution run free. It will be an exciting and wonderful time.

You can arrange a trial period of two to four weeks in a group. During this time, everyone can test each other socially and sexually and see whether they fit together. This is not about adaptation. Every human is unique. Determine if you can bring your uniqueness well into the group. If you are not quite sure about yourself yet, test it out and see what development opportunities the members of the group can give you. Determine how high the group's tolerance limit is and how high your own is. Does the social behavior fit? Pay particular attention to hygiene, alcohol, drugs. If the sexual possibilities are correct, you feel free in your decisions and the worldview also fits. Not everyone has to think and feel like you do, but can they also tolerate each other if you don't want to go along with everything? The others, in turn, can see how you fit into the group and thus enrich it. If that is true, then you will experience mutual love, trust, and help there.

In such a group a fantastic momentum develops in which you can realize yourself full of joy, just as our ancestors already experienced. But this fixed group offers many other advantages. It offers more security for the individual. A real extended family can emerge from this later. With children together who are brought up to be free and self-confident people. Ideally, a multi-generational family might emerge from this.

In such a community you will be more permanent, happier, and more content. Ideally, the group members will not have to adapt but can shape their personality and their life path more individually. This could be a way to a new, actually modified, better old, socially and sexually happy life, and slowly replace a marriage in its current permanent monogamous form to a large extent.

And one more thing at the end. I don't want to raise my index finger here, but I also have a certain responsibility in making these suggestions. During my research, I heard how young people, girls and boys alike, had group sex. That with elderly people, some of them strangers, and unprotected. I have seen guys in gay nude bars in Berlin how they were ecstatic with several men without restraint and wanted to test each other without protecting themselves. At first, I didn't want to believe it when I was told this until I saw it with my own eyes. I do not use such places for anonymous sex, whether homosexual, bisexual or heterosexual, for the reasons that have already been explained in detail. I couldn't imagine before those men who ought to know better would do this to inexperienced boys. But they did. But I also know that same-sex encounters with older strangers are not the norm. Even today there are already pills that protect against infection with HIV, better than any condom. But you should also take them before you test yourself uninhibited. I didn't know if these guys had taken it. I hope so.

The incumbent health minister in Germany is currently making this pill available to a "risk group" free of charge. I think that's the wrong signal. Why only one "risk group"? It can happen to anyone. Young people who want to test themselves or bisexuals do not go to the doctor and have themselves certified that they belong to a risk group. But it would be very beneficial for them to protect themselves with it. Also, the risk of infection with HIV is not limited to same-sex pleasure. From this point of view, it would then be the overwhelming part of the population that could be affected. So equal rights for everyone and without a prescription.

Most of the time something like this is experienced with a lot of joy and pleasure by the boys and girls. That was certainly a great experience. But very dangerous to health, especially with strangers. Certainly, there was alcohol involved, maybe drugs too. It is not innocent that adolescents have to suppress their strong sexual needs and reach for valves when they have the opportunity or have to look for them in complete secrecy. This is primarily not the fault of the adolescent, but of the social conditions and the wrong moral norms and rules in which they grew up.

Therefore, you have to take the responsibility yourself if you want to do better. More sexual self-determination always has something to do with more responsibility for yourself and others.

Therefore, it is essential to find out beforehand about the health consequences and how you can protect yourself against them. Also, talk about it in the group you might want to test. It is quite possible or likely that the members of the group are healthy and also outside of it, at least not having unprotected sex, if at all. Then you don't have to worry anymore and you can live it out without being pushed into anything. But don't take any risks and address the topic openly and honestly right from the start. Even if the stimulus and desire are so great and it is played down by others. Even the first time, you might suffer from damage to your health for a lifetime. That would mean the end of a really pleasurable and sexually fulfilled life until the end of your days. Do not be stupid. That shouldn't scare you now and keep you from a joyful, fulfilling youth life. If you have taken the necessary precautions, nothing can happen to you. But do it.

With changes in the social and family rules, this new way of living in groups would be entirely possible and would create a much better development opportunity for young people.

Of course, in today's world, because of school and training, it takes longer before young people can lead a financially independent life. But there is no reasonable reason why they cannot freely develop their sexuality and thereby their social experiences outside of the family. The emotional bond with the family will certainly not be disturbed, but the opposite will often be the case. Social rules and norms can be changed. Families can support their children on this path just as well as they have before.

Only that they give them greater personal responsibility, promote their free development opportunities, and thus make them more self-confident, happier people.

Epilogue

Young people have always been the engine of social change. And since they are to a large extent the victims of the bad social conditions for the free natural development of their lust and sexuality, they have the right to do something about it. But do not turn against the older generation in general, who live differently than you want them to. Find allies from among these ranks as well. Today they are sometimes more enlightened and open than they used to be. Talk about it in your family too. Your parents can allow you to live in a group as a "minor". You don't even have to change the laws right away.

One of the most important allies in the past has always been art. Here are a few examples of how you can make progress here:

Books and films

As a young or senior supportive writer or filmmaker, describe alternative ways of living. Not commercially, as usual, namely not how complicated and problematic they are, but how this enables a better and more fulfilling life. Don't be afraid to put your marriage aside. Also, don't hide the great natural sexual fulfillment and satisfaction in the group. To describe the love story of a group. Show the positive dynamics in such a community and so on. Show how teens feel in their sexual straitjacket. How they feel excluded from the family in their sexual development and how they thrive when they break free from it.

But it can also be built into other books and films such as crime novels and dramas. In historical topics, there have always been and have always been many bisexual relationships, which are mostly kept secret today, and other happy concepts of life. Most of the time, especially in historical topics, where the old scriptures are not interpreted, polygamous and bisexual ways of life can have a large, often positive part in historical development. Why are they always interpreted in a purely heterosexual direction? The other is just as beautiful and natural in human evolution. We need this understanding again.

Isn't it wonderful if David, in addition to his eight main wives, also had a deep and fulfilling sexual love affair with his friend Jonathan, which certainly brought about historical decisions? Or did Alexander the Great love his friend Hephaestion and spend many a pleasurable hour with him? Perhaps it was precise because of this that it positively influenced the motivation and strategy in this war of conquest? This can also be presented openly and as completely natural.

Here is an excerpt from Wikipedia:

"Similar to the Greek polis world south of Mount Olympus, same-sex love between males was widespread in ancient Macedonia and was largely socially accepted ... Historical research largely agrees that King Philip II of Macedonia, in addition to his numerous sexual relationships with women - he had among other things several wives - also had sexual contacts with men, especially courtiers. [34] [40] The later Greek and Latin authors Marcus Iunianus Iustinus, Curtius Rufus, and Athenaios von Naukratis also report in their writings of erotically connoted love affairs between his son Alexander and the Macedonian nobleman Hephaistion and the Persian courtier Bagoas. [41] [42] The majority of current researchers consider the aforementioned intimate relationships between Alexander and these two historical persons to be probable, despite a few opposing voices [43]"

The films that I know from Philipp and Alexander either leave this page out entirely or only make vague assumptions about it. They are only ever shown in relationships with women. The love between men was very widespread at that time and was noticeable in people's social life, certainly even in life decisions. Simply factoring that out gives the wrong picture of history. What effects did it have, for example, on the great stamina of his army, which had been on the road for many years and where same-sex love was socially recognized among each other? The same applies to the many film adaptations from ancient Greece, where bisexuality was also part of social normality and was even promoted. History is packed with these examples, and not just in ancient Greece and Macedonia.

The Queen of Sweden, Kristina, was also fond of a woman and had very progressive ideas for the time.

The story was worldwide and at all times sexual and in love much more colorful than it is usually played to us. Same-sex lustfulness between men and between women, as well as polygamy, were much more common in history than is shown today. It certainly had a positive effect on social conditions and thus on the development of societies and people. It would be very helpful if this page were displayed as something completely natural without a raised index finger. This serves to clarify our sexual historical development and leads us to ourselves.

And if it is supposed to be a romance novel or a film, then you could show that several people can love each other equally and are closely connected, including sexually. That was the rule for a long time. Historical facts were only twisted or kept secret in the orbit of the church, and many of them certainly still is today. It was the church that was the only institution to collect and translate historical documents for centuries. It determined which of them went public and which were kept secret and still are, even parts of the Bible. In particular, writings that reported a sexually free way of life were certainly not made available to the public by the church and are gathering dust in their secret archives to be able to keep their false teachings alive. We must finally end this nonsense because millions of people suffer from it.

Thankfully, however, the church did not get all of the scriptures into its hands. So today we know a lot about the Greeks, Macedonians, and Celts. But, likely, this is just a drop in the ocean. As a young person or the young at heart, you can help with your art to free people from prejudices and false beliefs. Help people to develop happily and freely again.

Music

Nothing carries new ideas faster than music. We know that from the hippie era. This music has evoked a new attitude towards life all over the world, especially among young people. That was the impetus for the sexual revolution and humanitarian child-rearing of that time. The public presentation of stars was and is a role model for many young people. Some of them professed their homosexuality or bisexuality even then. It would be good if the others also profess their natural bisexuality or their polygamy. Of course, this does not only apply to artists. You don't even have to say: "I am bisexual and polygamous", but it is enough to say that bisexuality and polygamy are a natural thing that is inherent in all or most people.

Support the final sexual liberation of young people from the long-outdated (un) moral ideas and the social norms and laws that still exist from them.

In songs, describe how underrated adolescents feel about their sexual development. How sexual desires and dreams are suppressed and why that is. Revolt against it. Sing of alternatives.

The music touches people's hearts and thus unfolds a tremendous power for change. Change the world and the completely inadequate moral concepts with music and lyrics. The time is ripe for it. You will be heard.

9. Bisexuality

As explained in the first chapters, same-sex pleasurable togetherness of people has been an integral part of their sexuality since the beginning of development. That was about a million years ago. All forms of sexuality were freely and openly lived out together. It then became equal normality around 300,000 years ago for Homo sapiens. Bisexual behavior by animals and Homo sapiens were dominant. This means that bisexuality can be seen as the most natural and original form of sexuality.

Through this long period, evolution could integrate this into physical development. As already described, in the course of evolution the pleasure points have been geared towards a bisexual life for men and women. This led to further development of the happy togetherness and strengthened the social bond in the group. Because these feelings and energies strengthened the person, gave him more motivation, and created a stronger, more stable connection with each other. From an evolutionary point of view, bisexuality is an advance in human development. In cultures where religions have not had much influence, it is still common practice today. They just keep a low profile from strangers who think differently about it.

In the past, the non-gender-specific orientation of sexual pleasure had many advantages in developing into the person we are today:

After the evolutionary development of all physical requirements, the feeling of pleasure was greatly expanded and led to more variety and possibilities.

The social ties between and within the sexes were thereby strengthened.

There was far less competition for the opposite sex.

As a result, equality between men and women was quite natural in social life. Both complemented each other perfectly. That led to faster and better further development. But that could essentially only develop in a firmly connected social group. So not with strangers or in a stable but tolerant two-way relationship.

Although many people sense or have at some point felt that it is in them too, they defend themselves against it, suppress it, or simply deny it to themselves. I have noticed this in many conversations.

Why is that?

The prejudices and false beliefs that have built up for thousands of years are still too strong for many to confidently walk this evolutionarily natural path. Nobody should force themselves to be bisexual. But you should also be honest with yourself. At the moment it can be assumed that many have this orientation, but deny it. But maybe you are heterosexual. Then, like purely homosexual people, you belong to a minority. But even that has no meaning and is natural.

The social environment usually does not tolerate it. That's what you're afraid of. However, if you are facing this fear, then you are the one bringing progress to your social group. I had a client who told me that when he was 24 when he confidently told his friends that he was bisexual. Little by little, almost all of his friends came to him and wanted to experience what it was like with him. Most of them enjoyed it very much.

You live in a monogamous two-way relationship, have these desires, but believe that the other will not accept it. Even a monogamous relationship in itself is questionable in the long run. Perhaps living out bisexuality together would be a better alternative. Preferably in a regular social group.

Although bisexuality used to be the social motor for development, it is difficult to live freely in today's conditions. Bisexual people get into conflict because they believe they have to choose something to feel part of it. But that is the completely wrong approach because they are in the overwhelming majority.

You are afraid of becoming homosexual. Only young men have these fears. As a rule, women do not have them. But homosexuality is also quite normal. So don't be afraid of it. Bisexuality used to be the rule and only a few chose the homosexual path. The pleasure with the same sex does not play a role in a one-sided sexual orientation. You don't become homosexual just because you are lustful with the same sex. And if you do realize that the same sex is more pleasurable for you, then you should be happy to have recognized it to live happier now.

To sometimes live out their bisexual side, many simply go from time to time to the currently prevailing homosexual subculture. There you can let off steam, but you can't identify with it and feel like an outsider. Both there and in a heterosexual social environment, you don't feel recognized. In the long run, this does not lead to a fulfilled sexual life.

Bisexuality used to be lived out in a social group of men and women by everyone and can thus lead to a more fulfilling and happier life. Of course, today it is also possible for men and women to live bisexually together in a group. Ideally, however, these should be socially connected, even if this does not always have to be permanent. You don't necessarily all have to live together. Today we have much better opportunities than our ancestors to be able to come together whenever we want.

Nevertheless, a stable community in a group would be optimal. Here this wonderful power of social bonding, complementation and help can best work on the development of each individual and thus lead to a better, more fulfilling life. If considered, children in such a group would grow up freer, happier, and more self-confident.

10. Homosexuality

Researchers are still working on the causes of homosexuality. Why? Is the direction you're looking for? It is much more likely that bisexuality was and is anchored in the genes of all human beings in the course of evolutionary development. In my opinion, homosexuality evolved from the bisexual relationships of primitive men.

It is easy to imagine that in primeval times there were not always groups in which the ratio of the sexes was balanced. Since bisexuality was known and used extensively for pleasure, it was only logical in a group with an unbalanced gender ratio that some turned more towards their gender, and at some point, they were exclusively active in it.

After thousands of years, bisexuality was anchored in people's genes and this also created the prerequisite that in general, the possibility of orientation could manifest itself in every person of the same gender. Depending on which sperm cell fertilizes the egg cell and under which instantaneous conditions cannot be influenced, this unambiguous, same-sex sexual orientation can occur even at birth. A particular gene that can be attributed to homosexuality and that one is looking for is unlikely to exist. It was a step forward for evolution to produce people with a same-sex orientation. Naturally, this has always existed in the animal kingdom.

Due to the bisexuality in the group, same-sex-oriented members were able to live out their lust to the fullest, even if they were alone in a clan with this clear orientation. So there was no need to develop a homosexual subculture. Bisexual men or women often favored them for the fulfillment of their desires. They had more experience in it to make lust the greatest pleasure in this way.

They were excluded from procreation and could therefore concentrate more on other things because they were not involved in the division of labor of a family. These men and women often worked as medicine men or women, later artists, philosophers, and politicians. They were often creative and drove progress. In this case, too, evolution has done a great job. Today it is estimated that around 10% of people are homosexual. According to the latest findings, the long assumed figure of 5% is outdated. It can be assumed that this percentage will increase with further evolutionary development.

Homosexual behavior comes in many forms. Today it is mostly described as explicit same-sex love between men, but for example in Venda, an area in South Africa, there was a system of women's weddings. And even among the women of the Arab-African Swahili population of Mombasa (Kenya), there was a social network of lesbian couples, here mostly between older and younger women. So homosexuality was and is not just a man's business. Today more and more lesbian couples appear in public and get married in Germany.

The Berliner Morgenpost reported in 2018:

Hundreds of gay and lesbian couples have already decided to get married in Berlin (since October of that year). From October to the end of December 680 couples tied the knot, as Interior Secretary Torsten Akmann (SPD) announced in response to a parliamentary request from the Greens in the House of Representatives. Around two-thirds of them were already living in a registered civil partnership. The "Tagesspiegel" had previously reported on it ... Two-thirds of them were men. (So a third woman)

Same-sex couples have been able to marry just like heterosexual couples since October 1st. Gays and lesbians had campaigned for this for decades, and the Bundestag cleared the way for it in the summer. Married homosexuals now have the same rights and obligations as heterosexual spouses, such as the right to adopt children.

We don't need marriage for everyone. Although under today's conditions it is important for social equality of same-sex love and thus a great victory for equality. Ultimately, it is just another reinforcement of this false, violent construct of what is called marriage. But sometimes something has to be recognized first before it can be rejected.

Despite the legal and thus social equality in some countries, homosexuals are unfortunately still extremely marginalized. Yes, in many countries homosexuality is still a criminal offense, up to the death penalty.

It works particularly well in people's minds. Even in an enlightened society, because it has still largely turned away from its natural, inherent bisexuality. These people are afraid of themselves. And that fear has been ingrained in them for two thousand years. In most cases, however, they did not lead a pleasurable, permanently fulfilled life. Fear creates resistance and hatred, which homosexuals then feel. And all because at some point, contrary to our natural disposition, it was banned.

Millions of people have died as a result of the course of this two-thousand-year history. This still affects today, even in a society in which homosexuality exists on an equal footing with other sexual relationships. Not only the opponents are to blame for this, but also some homosexuals themselves. Out of defiance, sex in public is provocatively exaggerated in the foreground to face the opponents with confidence. But this often turns them into exotic things for others, which they are not evolutionarily at all, and exclude themselves. But there are also more and more homosexuals who doubt that this is the right way to integrate.

What about the sexually fulfilled life in same-sex love in our country?

There are usually many options, especially for men in the big cities. The newly won freedom is enjoyed to the full. But this sometimes also leads to exaggerations, which do not have a favorable effect on a satisfying, lustful life. They meet in bars or discos. Most of the time there are also rooms in which they can hide as needed to give free rein to their lust.

Often they see their sex partner there for the first time or go alone into the darkroom and have lustful sex there anonymously. They seldom go home together and say goodbye to each other in the morning. There are online portals where you can arrange meetings and get down to business at the first meeting until you say goodbye after an hour or two. There are also nude discos, where they jump over each other on the open stage. All of these practices are very common. At least wherever there is a possibility. That is legitimate and human.

However, also superficially and over time the social and emotional bond to people with whom you are together in this wonderful way is missing. But that's an essential part of really happy and fulfilling sex life. Even homosexuals get lonely with this kind of uncomplicated acting out of their instincts and the possibly existing circle of friends never completely compensates for it. In the worst case, it makes you addicted to constant animal sex, the cause of which, however, is ultimately unsatisfied pleasure, which does not make you happy, but only makes you lonelier.

Of course, there are also homosexual couples who live together. This fixed connection is usually more open and usually leaves room for leeway to live out polygamous sexuality. Nevertheless, they love each other and often have very solid social and emotional ties. In their sex life with one another, they are usually active longer. The problem with this, however, is often that there are many uncomplicated opportunities, especially among men with the same sex orientation, to quickly get to know other interested parties. Even if it is only the search for a sexual adventure, in the beginning, feelings are aroused and you fall in love with someone else. In principle, that would not be a problem if these false beliefs about love had not been manifested in us for thousands of years. It is therefore often impossible to introduce the "newcomer" into a stable, long-term relationship as a third partner on an equal footing. So there has to be a decision. Either me or the other. So they often split up again. Therefore, there are very few permanent, permanent, homosexual relationships in which a life full of pleasure is possible.

Here, too, an alternative would be a shared apartment. It can consist of several homosexuals who fit together well and are fully satisfied with the way they live out their sexual needs within the group. Even when they get to know someone new, they can be more easily accepted into the group if everyone so wishes. However, a single homosexual can also join a larger, mixed group that lives bisexually. Here, too, he can find his permanent place and become very happy, as has been the case for thousands of years in a clan or extended family. In both cases, everyone will find more security and can live out their sexual desires much more often and better. This community is usually more stable and offers even larger and ideally further social contacts.

11. Masturbation - an emergency solution?

Masturbation is also observed more often in the animal kingdom and our ancestors certainly knew it too. It can be assumed, however, that in its time it was a method that was seldom used. On the one hand, they were used to freely satisfying their lust among each other, and on the other, they mostly stayed in groups. So there was no need for it. Seldom have there been situations at all where they were alone for a long time to have to satisfy their urges through masturbation. They lived together in a clan and also went hunting together. The sexually mature children were seamlessly included in the lustful hustle and bustle. So there was no reason for them to often satisfy their desires themselves. And since they were bisexual, everyone found one or more partners for it at all times.

The development of masturbation only took a turn with the introduction of the prohibitions in the writings of the Old Testament. Sex was only allowed in marriage, same-sex sex was forbidden, as was sex with animals. So people no longer had the opportunity to satisfy their strong sexual desires. This unnatural sexual deprivation was taken to extremes and even masturbation was banned. People had been put in an unbearable straitjacket. So everything was only done secretly and there was always the risk of being caught and punished. That could mean the death penalty at the time. Masturbation was the surest hidden way to avoid getting caught. And when she did, she wasn't punished so severely.

The tremendous pressure that people were under from such prohibitions resulted in more masturbation. But that too was always associated with fear and feelings of guilt. So it was mostly done clandestinely and quickly for the pure satisfaction of sexual pressure. A consciously deep, satisfying experience through personal self-awareness, as I will describe it later in this book, usually did not exist. It was never really satisfying and never led to a blissful state. Since the instincts could not be properly satisfied by this, it can be assumed that this is why it was carried out so often. Even in our time, masturbation is common. For one thing, even today sexually mature adolescents are not included in the full sexual life of adults. So they are compelled to spend the most beautiful and exciting years of their lust development with masturbation.

On the other hand, monogamous marriage is unsatisfactory in the long run, and attempts are made to weaken this through fantasies of masturbation. It is very likely that in a monogamous marriage, in the long run, significantly more orgasms are caused by masturbation than by sexual intercourse with the partner. And let's not forget the increasing single culture. However, masturbation, especially if it lasts, is always an indication of unsatisfactory sex life. It indicates that our sex life is not or cannot be lived out naturally.

If so, let's make the best of it, some enterprising people told themselves. And so a whole industry came into being for this need. Dildos for women of all sizes and with all technical refinements, anal dildos for men to stimulate their pleasure zone, porn books, magazines, films, something for really everyone: phone sex and live sex on the Internet, where you can watch and express your wishes and much more.

In Germany, around 47 million euros are only spent on pornographic material each year, and the trend is rising. With phone sex, more than two billion euros are sold worldwide each year. Phone sex is on the decline, but new forms are being offered on the Internet to make masturbation more pleasant. Here, too, there is no deep inner satisfaction, at most a brief relief. This can even lead to sex addiction, especially in young men and women.

It's an addiction like any other. Initial feelings of happiness disappear quickly and turn into uncontrolled, increasingly stronger, tormenting desire. It leads to loneliness and the personality is gradually destroyed. All ethical and moral principles are pushed aside when it serves to satisfy an addiction.

It starts especially with young people who have not yet had sex and who have to masturbate for years. It is, therefore, no wonder that more and more young people have problems with potency. I also know that from practice. These can be fears, erection problems, listlessness, and orgasm difficulties. Young, potent people, whose whole life lies ahead of them, come to me with potency problems due to our social conditions. That should make us think.

Of course, in our time, masturbation doesn't always have to be a stopgap solution. In stressful times, we sometimes want to be alone with ourselves and our lustful feelings. It just depends on what you make of it. That's why I'll give you a little guide later in this book.

12. Looking into the future from the past

When humans stepped out of the animal kingdom, they began to reflect on their environment. So he became more and more aware of his instincts. As with all living beings, these instincts produced the strongest and most intense feelings of happiness. But the man saw in them a means to become happier in life as a whole. Of course, he now used them more diversely and no longer just for reproduction. With this, he developed a new social consciousness, from which later natural and non-possessive, polygamous love emerged. Since he was bisexual like all living beings, he had every opportunity to establish pleasurable and social connections.

Sex and pleasurable togetherness became an integral, inseparable part of living together. In this way, we strengthened social relationships and built new ones. And we lived that out freely and openly for a long time. It was this wonderful happiness and there were no rules or norms. It was a development process that was also supported evolutionarily by physical development to be able to experience sexual feelings more intensely and more diversely.

That made sense for evolution because it advanced our development. Through these blissful, strong feelings, we strengthened our bonds and relationships with both sexes in a wonderful, beautiful, and strong way. Through this inner satisfaction, the deepest connections with other people, and the strengthening of body and soul, our consciousness was able to develop further. Sex has become a driving force in human development and human society. With the advent of religions, which began around 3,000 years ago, this process was interrupted and misdirected. This had dramatic consequences on our further sexual development and also hurt our consciousness development, especially in our social behavior. Even today we are under this influence to a greater extent than we realize.

Be it the pleasurable games of the children, the first sexual experiences of the adolescents in all possible ways, the pleasurable experience with another person outside of a fixed relationship, the masturbation, the same-sex sexual experience, the erotic relationship with animals and trees. Much is done secretly today and creates more or less guilty feelings. It prevents us from a free natural development of sexual pleasure and the diverse and enriching social bonds that result from it.

But that determines our attitude towards life and is a guarantee for a happy and fulfilled life. A million years of evolution cannot be erased in 3,000 years. We humans carry everything in us and feel what makes us happy. We just have to do it freely again and be able to enjoy it.

The removal of humans from the reproductive process is the result of evolution. It will continue to develop. A completely natural development process that is understandable and logical. Through self-determination about his sexuality and the social stability associated with it, man multiplied until he populated the whole planet. It would only be a matter of time before this process collapses if this continued. The release of sexual pleasure from procreation was also necessary to secure human existence in the long term. Sex was given a qualitatively higher function. The diversity in the fulfillment of lust, especially in same-sex love, was a natural impetus for the future development of man. As a result, the birth rate remained stable for thousands of years. In the Stone Age, 10 000 years ago, the number of people, which was probably constant for thousands of years, was estimated at 5 million worldwide. But then religion came and reversed this development of sexual diversity. Sex was only allowed for reproduction and the population exploded. First, three thousand years ago, it was the Jews who introduced this restriction. The population rose to 250 million by the turn of the times. In the first few centuries, it rose only slowly, which up to the 18th century could be explained by disease epidemics and wars. Plague, famine, and wars often halved the population in Europe again. One can also assume that mother earth resisted the rise of humanity on her, as they moved more or less more and less parasitically on her. But then it rose explosively and from around one billion in the 18th century to around three billion in 1950, although there, too, there were two world wars in between.

Of course, the increase in population cannot be explained by religion alone. Many aspects of social development worldwide play a role, but I cannot go into them here. I am only looking at what influence religion and social changes had on human sexual development. In 1987 there were 5 billion people on earth. In 2017 it was 7.6 billion and by 2100 the forecasts predict 11.18 billion. Here, too, people will find solutions. Besides, people are getting older. But how long will it go on like this? Without the intervention of evolution, this will not be possible in the long term. It created the conditions three hundred thousand years ago. The sexual feelings will become further removed from the reproductive instinct. You will transform yourself into something higher and lustfully become an ever stronger social force and not in lifelong monogamy and restriction to one gender. Both in short-term or permanent two-way relationships and groups.

The sexual and social evolutionary process will continue. And if we follow him, wonderful things will await us that we cannot even imagine today. In my energy work and in the bioenergetic massage I developed, I have already been able to gain a deeper insight into it. Although it wasn't about sex, I got very hopeful feedback. Often this was followed by spontaneous exclamations like: "That was better than any sex I've had before." Or: "I've never experienced anything like this before."

How strong would the sexual ecstasy be if we could release these energies and feelings that are already within us? This shows me that much deeper feelings of happiness are still waiting for us to be discovered and set free. Yes, which will certainly evolve to further strengthen and intensify our social relationships. Maybe even, at some point, in a completely new and out-of-body way. On the way of the blissful, ecstatic, and orgasmic feelings they are always evoked, they will increase our consciousness and our social cohesion. The reproduction will no longer play a role. At some point, this will allow us to enter a qualitatively new evolutionary phase. I am convinced that this is the goal of evolution and the free development of our wonderful sexual energy and strength is a crucial key to it. Therefore, in the next chapter, I will give you some suggestions on how we can make our sex life more pleasurable.

13. Methods to significantly increase pleasure and to resolve sexual problems in adolescents and adults

The ways of life forced upon us, but also the stress of our time, very often lead to mental and physical problems. They can significantly reduce or disturb our sexual desire and its fulfillment. More and more people, young and old, are therefore resorting to drugs that are supposed to reduce or even remedy this. This is now a billion-dollar business. However, these drugs also have strong side effects and are therefore usually not suitable for a fulfilling and above all healthy sex life. Especially since there are other and sometimes more effective, natural methods. In this section, I'll introduce you to some of them.

The advantage of these natural methods lies in their holistic effect. By increasing the feeling of pleasure in this way, you also reduce stress, dissolve mental blockages and strengthen the whole body. This will permanently and naturally make your sex life more beautiful and fulfilling.

13.1. Through masturbation to a full-body orgasm

With masturbation, you can experience yourself. They test how they can achieve the greatest feelings of pleasure and increase their orgasm experience to previously unimagined heights.

Find an undisturbed, quiet place for it. A place where you feel comfortable. Most of all, take your time. If you are short on time, then leave it completely, because in the short term you will find at most a brief relief, but not ascend into the blissful realm of pleasure, which brings you deep satisfaction. Turn off anything that distracts you and then focus only on your body and your emotions.

When you have created the right conditions, relax and consciously adjust to your body and your sensual feelings. Most do best when they close their eyes. Then start caressing your body, especially all the lustful areas on it. Often they discover zones that they were not even aware of before.

Everyone has their special pleasure zones. Caress your body and find out. Mostly it is the ears, the neck, the nipples, the stomach, the inside of the thighs, the buttocks, the anus, and directly the sex. Take your time and enjoy every lustful place. Enclose your whole body in a single pleasure field with your caresses.

When you've done that, slowly begin to increase your arousal by stimulating your private parts more. Here, too, the journey is the goal. Enjoy these feelings that become more intense over time. Feel these wonderful energies flow through your whole body. Stay completely relaxed and do it slowly but unstoppably, getting stronger and stronger. Enjoy this incessant, ascending lust. Do not take a break.

Start moaning with surrender. Say: "Oh, that's nice, yes go on, go on!" Stimulate yourself slowly but without interruption. It's getting more and more intense. You feel an orgasm building inside you. You feel it very intensely. You feel this feeling slowly rising inexorably and it is almost unbearable. Now your stimulation will slow you down so that you can enjoy this moment of highest pleasure for as long as possible.

But then it explodes inside you. As you do this, try to relax your body and let yourself go. Through a relaxed body, these uniquely strong, indescribably beautiful, orgasmic feelings can flow deep into it. Feel how these ecstatic feelings run through your whole body. You moan loudly and this moan comes out of you very deeply. If you did it right, you have just had a tremendous full-body orgasm and find deep, happy contentment in it.

Try out different body positions! Your imagination has no limits. In most cases, widely spread legs have proven effective for both women and men. Do it lying down and sometimes standing. When standing, lean comfortably against a wall with one side of your shoulder. Stand with one leg on a chair. In this way, you can easily access all of your erogenous zones. The best posture can make your orgasm even more powerful. Try it out! In this way, you get to know and control your body and your orgasm behavior better and better. You can then also use this for pleasurable activities with others to experience one full-body orgasm after the other.

By inducing this quiet, powerful orgasm, men let some of their semen in and can climax more often. Practice it. It is worth it. If you then do it in pairs, talk calmly at the beginning about what you want and how, because you have explored it all in detail. In this way, you can make your sex life a lot nicer and more often.

Last but not least, you will be showered with a larger amount of happiness hormones, which are good for your body and soul. Even with sexual listlessness and frigidity, you can increase your sensation of pleasure again. This also applies to orgasm difficulties.

13.2. The first time

Unfortunately for many young people, it is not as enjoyable the first time as they imagined. You are disappointed and therefore hold back for further experiences for the time being. Most of the time this happened under the influence of alcohol or drugs. Then they lose their inhibitions. Alcohol is consumed consciously to loosen up. But that's the wrong way. Take this step without clouding your consciousness. The first time you do it with someone you are attracted to, who you find sexy, who you know, and whom you trust. It doesn't necessarily have to be "great love". In general, however, you should protect yourself with condoms when uniting. So, boys and girls, take enough condoms with you! Create a nice atmosphere for yourself and your partner in a place where you are undisturbed. Plan a lot of time for this.

Foreplay is always important. Kisses, hugs, caresses. But especially the erotic parts of the body should be stimulated as much as possible. Don't be shy. You will certainly make the other happy with it. Forget the old notions of active and passive! It gets nice when both are actively involved. Sometimes girls are even more anxious than boys. It's natural because something new is happening for them. If they are still a virgin, they will lose their virginity. This is still a decisive event for many today.

Open yourself! You too can do what you imagined beforehand in your imagination. Check out your partner's nudity. Explore his body with your hands and with kisses. Tell the boy what you feel like doing right now. Ask him to do what you want right now. That creates trust and security for both. Ask what the other wants and then do it with a lot of passion.

Boys are usually very aroused from the start and are afraid of orgasm prematurely, which often happens. That too is quite natural. But it's not bad. On the contrary, it can be very beneficial. So don't suppress it, but let it come joyfully. After that orgasm, your body is full of happiness hormones. Just keep on caressing each other. That feels good. In the next 10 to 20 minutes you will usually have the next erection and can now go a step further if the girl is ready and wants it now. To do this, continue to stimulate her pleasure points and especially her clitoris beforehand. She will then be ready and let you in for the first time. Do this carefully. After your first orgasm, you will have a better grip on your passion and you will be able to focus more on your partner's lust.

Don't go all the way in either. But always just a little bit in and out. That increases the girl's lust. As a girl, you should be active now. When you feel you're ready, push against it and push the boy's limb further inside you. Then determine the rhythm with your movements and show how it should go on. Or tell the boy: "Faster, slower, deeper, harder or not so tight." If you feel like it, turn around and sit on him. Then you can completely determine what happens. Your partner will love it. And if he wants, he'll turn you on your back after a while and you can open yourself up to him again. Since he has already had an orgasm, the second time it usually takes longer before he comes back and needs a break. That's nice like that. This allows both of your lust to develop fully the first time. Even as a girl, you can have one or more orgasms the first time.

Don't stop right after that. But kiss each other and continue to give each other tenderness. Your happiness hormones are now flowing through your body at full speed. With more caresses and stimulations, you can let them romp for a while. If you both feel great lust again, don't hold back.

The more intense and orgasmic the first time, the more joy you will have with it in the future. In the end, gently caress the whole body of your partner and enjoy this wonderful experience in your imagination, which had just overwhelmed you. It's a myth that guys or men always want to quit right after orgasm. They too can learn to continue enjoying their feelings of happiness afterward. If you do this the first time, it will continue to work.

The first time with the same sex

The same applies, of course, when young people of the same sex have a pleasurable experience for the first time. Again, foreplay is very important. It's not that difficult with girls. Kisses and tender touches are easier for them. Girls usually know their erotic spots. And the orgasmic act can be done in different ways. For example, by rubbing the bodies in a position where they can easily reach their mutual pleasure points. Some drawings are thousands of years old. But also caressing or kissing each other with the tongue in the most pleasurable places, such as the nipples and clitoris, can lead to an orgasmic climax.

Here, too, do not stop immediately when you have reached the climax, but also exchange tenderness with each other afterward. Most of them often find this game among girls to be very familiar. You can play it as long as you like and don't have to worry about the boy's orgasm, which happens faster and then needs a while to rest. Girls don't need that rest afterward. That is why they sometimes find each other very pleasurable. It can always lead to one orgasm or more. Boys, on the other hand, often test same-sex sex on their anus alone. That is also quite normal. Most guys find it very exciting when they imagine this. As already explained, this is probably in our genes and is therefore quite natural. Most of the time, however, they test it alone, without much foreplay or tenderness, with their fingers or other objects and are then disappointed. Here, too, you need a partner you can trust and feel an attraction to. But first, be tender to one another. Touch and kiss. You will notice very quickly that it is also very nice with a boy and that it excites you. Again, a quick orgasm is no reason to stop. Just keep going. The pleasure comes back quickly.

If you then want to offer or take the "blossom of your body", to speak with the Greeks, full of pleasure, then it is also important to prepare the union with pleasurable foreplay. Caress and kiss the flower. Use some oil or cream the first time. Massage this bud gently and passionately. This is how your partner will open up further. If it opens further, feels free to put your finger in a little. Soon you will notice a slightly harder point. This is the prostate, also known as the man's G-spot. Then you rub it gently and your friend becomes extremely excited. Wait until he tells you to get inside him now.

Then slowly and carefully with your hard member in and out, always a little deeper. Here, too, there is no active and passive. Both can determine the rhythm. You can do that best the first time in the so-called "doggy position". One of them crouches on all fours in front of the others. By rubbing the pleasure point on the prostate with the excited member, both will gradually experience the highest feelings of happiness. He can do the same to you afterward. Here, too, caresses afterward and further exploration of the body is nice. If you feel like doing it again, the whole thing can be repeated at will and the positions can also be changed again. It doesn't matter if you do it more often the first time and let off steam. So plan a lot of time for it and choose an undisturbed location for it.

Again, boys or girls don't lose lust just because they can experience the most beautiful feelings with the same sex. It doesn't matter whether you do it more often or regularly. Unless, from the outset, they were primarily or exclusively geared towards the same gender. If not, they will only enrich their pleasurable, exciting life and create stronger social connections with both sexes. Sex is not something to be ashamed of, it should be enjoyed and confident about it. If you want, you can try this possibility without hesitation. Everything is permissible and natural as long as no one is forced to do so or made compliant by alcohol and drugs. Humans have the largest shoots between the ages of 16 and 18. So enjoy this lust in your youth. It gives you a tremendous boost. You will be much happier and more balanced. Use this happiness in you to achieve your other goals as well. Be it at school, at university, or work. That will also be much easier for you then.

13.3. Natural remedies to strengthen the feeling of pleasure

Eat a healthy diet. I am not writing that here because it is so mandatory to write about natural nutrients and their positive effects, but because I and my clients have realized that it is very important in our time to approach them with respect, think highly of them. And not only what food you eat, but you also have to pay attention to the quality. By now everyone knows that cheap meat, fruit, and vegetables don't contain many nutrients if they don't even contain toxins.

Also, avoid sweets. We usually consume far too much sugar, which also hurts our sex life. Although chocolate is said to have an aphrodisiac effect and this has been confirmed to me on several occasions, eat it with care. If you like, go for tart chocolate with a high cocoa content. It has less sugar and it is the cocoa that causes this effect anyway. But other foods have this effect. If you don't want to miss out on sweet things, then eat fruit. Most types of fruit are potency-enhancing.

Hot spices such as chili also have a potency-promoting effect. I would like to tell a little story about this:

When I was in Asia on business, I naturally wanted to get to know the varied and delicious dishes that I had heard a lot about. The first few days I was invited to the restaurant. The food was always very tasty, but it didn't differ much from my favorite restaurant in Germany. So I expressed the wish to get to know the original Asian cuisine one day. Immediately two men invited me and took me to their local pub. It wasn't a pub, but rather an old, large garage. There were wooden folding benches and tables. Older women prepared the food in bulging pans and pots against one wall and offered it for sale.

After looking at the food that was laid out there in sequence and past fried bugs, grasshoppers, maggots, chicken legs, and other indefinable foods, I saw something in a red sauce that looked like chicken. My companions confirmed that it was chicken. So I took a portion of it with rice. There were napkins at the end of the table. Very classy, I thought. Since I looked skeptical and wasn't sure that it was chicken, my companions also took it but got a bag with fried bugs and maggots as a snack. When I started to eat, my mouth stayed open. It was indescribably sharp. I immediately started sweating. After the third bite, the sweat poured down my face. I got a pack of napkins to keep wiping myself clean. My companions enjoyed themselves deliciously. I couldn't eat much of it and only stuck to the rice, which was excellent.

After my companions finished eating, they laughed at each other, looked at me, and pointed down. I saw that they both got erections while eating. Immediately I protested and asked why I didn't have that too. They laughed again and explained that it was the sharpness that did it. That was also logical for me. The heat got the circulation going and led to an erection. I just couldn't eat the spicy food.

At the next table sat three rather old men. I asked my companions if they could get an erection while eating. They just smiled sweatily and shrugged their shoulders. They didn't know either and I didn't dare go to them to see. My companions told me to eat my meat so that I could get an erection too. I didn't, it was just too hot for me and proudly said that we Europeans don't need something like that. We would also have so much strength and endurance. Then all three of us laughed.

Hot spices such as chili and the like are certainly also potency-enhancing. But if you want an immediate effect, you have to eat a lot of spicy food. I learned that back then.

Anyone interested in aphrodisiac foods and drinks will find countless pages about them on the Internet. But be careful: Not everything that is written there is correct and some things are also not entirely harmless. At this point, I would like to introduce the substances with which I have had good experiences with my clients and in some cases also with myself.

Ginseng

Ginseng is sometimes offered as a potency-enhancing plant, but it has many other effects on the whole body and therefore generally helps to slow down the aging process. No other plant has been tested and studied as thoroughly as this one. Its beneficial effect in many ways has been proven. For many of my clients, ginseng had a positive effect on potency. Due to the general strengthening of the body, the increase in energy and well-being, it can be assumed that it can also have a positive effect on the feeling of pleasure in women.

Make sure, however, that the amount of ginsenosides is specified in a standardized way. There should be at least 50mg per capsule. You can then take one or two of these a day. It should also be Red Panax Ginseng. This is the most effective and comes from Asia, most certainly from Korea. There are many reliable and reliable reports on the Internet about the broad spectrum of effects of ginseng. If you want, you can find out more there.

Please also note that this is a natural plant and not a medicine. So it takes a certain amount of time to work. Allow two to four weeks for it to work. In any case, it has a positive effect on you on the first day. In young people, however, it sometimes affects their erection behavior after two to three days, with partially resounding success. Young people should therefore not take ginseng all the time but should stop using it for two to three months after three to six months. Don't worry, the effect will last.

Ginko

Ginko makes the blood more fluid. The blood flow to the body improves, which can be positive for pleasure and erection. In particular, it increases potency when taking ginseng at the same time.

In medicine, Ginkgo is used to improve brain performance. Only Ginkgo Biloba is used here. It can also delay or prevent age-related degenerative diseases in the brain. There are enough studies on this. It is also used medicinally for ringing in the ears. But it also has a powerful antioxidant effect. That is, it fights aggressive molecules that can attack and destroy your body cells. Ginkgo also helps with headache and tinnitus, erectile dysfunction and asthma, with circulatory disorders and arteriosclerosis.

Further information is available at https://www.ginkgo-ratgeber.info/

Make sure that the preparation contains a standardized amount of ginkgo flavone glycosides. 120 mg ginkgo extract should contain at least 24% of it. This once-a-day dose should be enough. In the case of higher doses, for example, to delay degenerative diseases, you should consult a doctor beforehand. There are many offers on the market. Compare the quality offered with the price. For young people, the same rule applies here, again and again, to take a break for two or three months.

Omega 3

Omega 3 fatty acids are most commonly found in fish oil capsules. For vegetarians, however, they are also available on a plant basis. Although they are recommended for many ailments, the reference to potency enhancement is not directly listed. However, I have noticed this effect very often with my clients, and indeed noticeably. Well worth checking out. Omega 3 fatty acids also have a wide range of positive effects. Virtually every area of your body needs substances that depend on an adequate supply of omega 3 fatty acids.

Make sure you are consuming a total of at least 1000 mg total of EPA and DHA per day for full effect. "1000 mg omega 3 fatty acids" alone is not enough. The specification of EPH and DHA must be stated on the packaging. If it doesn't work after a few weeks, try another provider. It is amazing how different these preparations work with the same content. There are probably big differences in quality. Fish oil capsules are also suitable in lower doses for children and during pregnancy. Teenagers should take them permanently. Unless it has too strong a potency-promoting effect. I had a young man who kept getting erections as a result. He then stopped taking it and later successfully continued it with a lower dose. With today's diet, it is hardly possible to get a sufficient amount of omega 3.

With these natural remedies, you can, under certain circumstances, greatly improve your potency and your sexual pleasure. A more intense orgasm experience in women and men is often reported. The biggest benefit is that you strengthen your whole body and mind at the same time. That means you have a lasting natural effect and probably a long, fulfilling sex life ahead of you.

Good sex needs a healthy body. Due to our poor diet, which is based on our eating habits, but also the deterioration of the food, I recommend taking a good, all-encompassing spectrum of nutrients besides in the form of a multi-preparation. There is an infinite number of these on the market and many are as good as ineffective. So here are some tips on how to identify a good preparation.

What special ingredients, besides the usual vitamins and minerals, should you find in a multi-preparation?

It should contain a sufficient amount of vitamin C. I take one with 500 mg of vitamin C.

Natural vitamin E at least 100 IU

There should be enough D3 in it. At least 1000 IU

All vitamin B complexes should be several times higher than the minimum dose.

Zinc at least 15 mg in the form of zinc glucose.

Chromium at least 200 mcg in the form of chromium picolinate.

Folic acid at least 400 mcg

If you pay attention, you have a good multi-supplement. Usually, there are also calcium and magnesium in there. However, the dosage does not have to be 100% of the daily requirement, as you can get this well with a balanced diet. Iron is also not necessary, and can even be harmful if you do not suffer from iron deficiency.

13.4. Suggestive programming for a noticeable increase in pleasure. Even with sexual disorders.

Wrong beliefs and blockages that arose from experiences were sometimes firmly transported into your deep consciousness. They unconsciously influence your feelings and decisions. Sometimes your body too. This can have very negative effects on your sexual development and fulfillment that you cannot change with just your thinking. To do this, you have to go into your deep consciousness yourself. To do this properly, there are a few rules that need to be followed. For this, I have developed various hypnoses, one of which I would like to present to you for use in self-hypnosis. In my book "Become the Creator of Your Life" I have already given a detailed explanation of self-hypnosis. In this book, however, I must repeat a few things.

There are many ways to get into hypnosis. Here I am describing a way into hypnosis that I have already used hundreds of times and how it works equally well for self-hypnosis.

How quickly you then get into hypnosis is very different. Some practice may be necessary, especially in self-hypnosis. While everyone can visualize, some find it difficult to do so consciously. It just takes a little practice. When you have become a professional, and I have no doubt that you can become one, it often only takes a few seconds and you no longer have to use the route that I will describe to you later.

The place for your suggestion

Find a place for self-hypnosis where you feel comfortable. Many prefer a quiet room in which they feel safe and secure. A room, perhaps with objects that mean a lot to you. A room in which you can feel a lot of positive energies. This room doesn't have to be dark. On the contrary, it is usually more pleasant to be in a light-flooded room. Others prefer an outside space. Here you feel free and can relax best. Test it out if you can.

In my coaching room, I placed particular emphasis on colors, images, and energy symbols. With lots of light, wood, and pleasant smells.

The body position in the suggestion

Assume a posture that makes you feel completely relaxed. Please remember that you have to hold this position for a longer period without it being pinched or uncomfortable. Many people cross their arms behind their heads or place them on their chests when lying on their backs. In the long run, this becomes uncomfortable in deep relaxation. It is best to put your arms on your side. Also, make sure that you don't freeze while doing this. Even if it doesn't seem necessary to you at the beginning, cover yourself up. Some feel more relaxed in an armchair. Just try it out for yourself. Later you can then simply perform the self-hypnosis in any position.

In my coaching room, I use an adjustable, very soft massage bench. Here I can adjust the lying position individually.

Other environmental factors in the suggestion

As a rule, it should be a quiet room. Avoid annoying noises from outside. With more and more practice, however, it will no longer bother you and you can relax that deeply. Give your room good fragrances that you like. Sounds to support hypnosis are often offered via MP3 and CD. Test whether they seem helpful to you. Conversations that we have with ourselves in self-hypnosis (as discussed below) will usually be disruptive.

The right time for suggestion

For self-hypnosis, I recommend choosing a time when you are awake and rested. Usually, this is in the morning after washing and before breakfast. Start the day relaxed and with new energy. This morning's hypnosis doesn't have to take long. Maybe 15 to 20 minutes. Later, 5 to 10 minutes are enough. If possible, do this two to three times a week for a while. Take the time to do it.

You will see that it is worth it. In hypnosis, you will quickly find the rituals that will help you to dive into your deep consciousness without spending any further time.

When dealing with larger problems, you need more time in the beginning. If you can't find the time to do this in the morning, you'll have to find another time. In this case, it is important to go into hypnosis without time pressure. But you shouldn't be tired there either, or you'll fall asleep.

If I notice in my coaching practice that a client is tired, I do some energetic physical exercises with them to revive them. For example, I let him wiggle his hips around the room for a few minutes. You can do that at home too.

When you have prepared everything, you can start relaxing:

Go into self-hypnosis

Lie down relaxed and close your eyes. Position your arms loosely next to your body, breathe in and out very calmly. Make sure that with each exhale, you get heavier and lower and lower. Tell yourself in your mind: "The deeper I sink, the more comfortable and relaxed I feel."

You will feel yourself becoming more and more relaxed as you do so.

Put yourself in your mind now to a place you know, where you are very happy and where you feel particularly comfortable and safe. It can also be a fantastic place. The more unrealistic the place where you feel comfortable, the deeper you go into hypnosis. But it should just be a place that you will be happy to come back to with every further hypnosis.

Try to see this place in front of you like in a dream. Take a look around, the contours are slowly becoming clearer and clearer. You may hear birds and smell flowers. Sometimes it helps if you look at a nice place on a picture beforehand or smell a flower or perfume. Relax. You are now in another, spiritual world or, if you will, in your dream world, and everything is possible there.

Arrive in deep awareness

In this place, you will see a comfortable wide lounger. You go to this couch and lie down on it. It's very soft and comfortable. You are now lying on this soft, comfortable lounger in the middle of your favorite place. That feels wonderful. You feel free and safe.

With this lounger, you can now slowly and calmly go deeper and deeper. The deeper you sink, the freer and safer you feel. Deeper and deeper down. You pass an invisible gate. You will feel a small but pleasant resistance and then you will sink again very deeply. That's nice. You are now in a bright, beautiful corridor. It is the passage of your depth consciousness. They walk down the aisle. There are doors on the right. You walk past the doors. The further you go, the better you will feel. Now stop at a door. You turn to this door and see a sign on it. This sign says "Room of Emotions". You read it again: "Room of feelings."

You open this door and stand on a summer meadow, stand in the green grass, and see the colorful flowers. Red poppies, blue bluebells, yellow buttercups. You can see how colorful butterflies flutter across the meadow. You stand in the middle of the meadow and breathe the fresh, oxygen-rich air. You feel infinitely free and happy.

Now, look around. You look across the meadow and see a large single tree in the middle of the meadow. It is your tree of life with a thick trunk and a green crown of leaves. You go to that tree and hug the big trunk. You press your whole body firmly against the trunk and feel a slight vibration. You feel your life energy. This energy is now going into your body. You feel pleasant warmth that spreads throughout your body. You will feel a pleasant, light-tingling sensation all over your body. You feel the energy that strengthens your body. That feels good. You feel strong and free now. Now you detach yourself from your tree and have arrived with in-depth consciousness.

Now you can just let go. Let go of people, beliefs, prejudices, and more. Also, think about people you don't have a good relationship with.

Then say the following sentences:
1. I forgive you.
2. I bless you.
3. I love you and let go.

To 1. Forgiveness comes first because this is the only way to let go of someone or something. In other words, if I still have a grudge against someone who wronged me or made me angry or sad, then I carry it around with me. I have to forgive the other person and thus get rid of the negative feelings that are only keeping me from my happiness.

To 2. With the blessing, one feels the power to be able to bless someone or something. You feel like a creator. That feels good. You don't have to be a believer to bless someone. You just have to do it. That is not a privilege of religion, anyone can do it. Everyone is a part of creation and can bless whoever they want. Prejudices and false beliefs have also been a part of you up to now. So bless them too.

I bless you in the name of creation that we are both made of. Everything is connected. When I bless you, I am blessing creation and myself. Do you feel the tremendously positive power behind it?

To 3. If you still love someone who has broken up with you, then you should say that too, not lie. Nevertheless, one lets go of the other and surrenders them to the universe. If the two of you belong together, then you can only find yourself anew once you let go. If you do not belong together, then you have let go, you feel free, you are open to other people and also to love.

When you have had enough practice, you can shorten this path and go straight to the meadow near your tree of life. If you try it out and notice that it doesn't really work out yet, lengthen the path again. Don't put yourself under pressure. It's just a matter of time without compulsion. But always start in the meadow and hug the tree of life. Feel the energy and recharge yourself with it. This is the prerequisite for the success of all further steps.

From this location, you can now convey your concerns into your deep consciousness and quickly and unadulterated reach the universal consciousness.

There is a second option that some may find particularly helpful. I would like to introduce these to you. Just try what is best for you.

So here is another expansion option:

After you have absorbed energy in your tree of life and have arrived in your deep consciousness, you will meet a companion on the meadow. An angel or someone you made up someone from the past who is very important to you, or someone whose body has already died and whom you know or who you adore. That can also be a great personality from history. Spiritual people can also add their power animal. Regardless, it is a companion from your deep consciousness.

So a direct contact. This accompanying you on your journey through your depth consciousness and your desires. They may just look on at you in a friendly and confident manner, show you pictures, or have a chat with them. Try it.

Let us now come to your wish for a fulfilling, sexually pleasurable life.

Carrying out self-suggestion
"Go into relaxation as usual and then into your depth of consciousness."

In the beginning, it is helpful to use the three stages described for this. So the relaxed inhalation and exhalation lead you deeper and deeper into relaxation. Your favorite place to start visualizing and feeling. The lounger that, like an elevator, brings you further down into your deep consciousness. Finally, the embrace of your tree of life, which connects you emotionally with deep awareness.

Then you stand by your tree of life on the meadow and see your companion. You feel a great pleasure doing it. Walk up to him and hug him happily as you greet him. Your companion is the symbol of your depth consciousness and this is how you should feel it. You have made direct contact with this. In everything that happens now, you will be accompanied and strengthened by deep awareness.

Your companion enters your body from behind and fills it with warmth and energy. It is now in the body. You feel it in you. You feel its energy. It feels very good and familiar. You will feel how this energy strengthens every single cell in your body. You feel it, starting from your feet and moving upwards. It's warm and comfortable. If you have any health problems, it will be very warm at this point. This warmth stays in this place for a short time until you feel really good. Then it goes on. Sometimes it gets warmer where you don't feel a problem. But you admit it and enjoy this wonderful intimate union with your companion. You feel the healing and lustful energy. Your companion leaves your body again, this time at the front. You are full of happiness and love. You hug him and he hugs you. You thank him for this wonderful strengthening of your body and your emotions.

It is a targeted activation of your body through your depth awareness and the language of feelings. Always let your companion enter from behind and exit from the front. It has been shown that the process in the body and the subsequent result can be better emulated and felt.

You can also do this strengthening or healing process separately. When you have learned to go into your depth consciousness quickly, you can always use it for just a minute or two. Just let your helper in. no matter where you are. It works better than any energy drink or some medicine. But don't forget to be grateful at the end of the day. This will make you feel connected to your deep awareness and the exercise will not fail to have its effect.

Next, you walk hand in hand with your companion across the meadow to a beam of light that hits the meadow vertically from above. It's so big that you can lie down in it. Your companion asks you to get into it, whatever you do. You are completely enveloped in the light and feel safe. Now you will notice how they begin to slowly float upwards in the beam of light. You look down and see how the meadow is slowly moving further and further away from you. You feel completely safe and secure in this beam.

Now you can see how shadows sink onto the meadow. There you dissolve. Now you notice these shadows are coming from your back. You are now watching how you release yourself from your back. Every time a shadow comes off your back you will feel a slight tingling sensation and afterward you will feel good. Always better and lighter, with every shadow that loosens. Until they all come out of you and float down to where they dissolve. Now look up again and see a big light at the end of the beam. They are getting closer and closer and the light is getting bigger and bigger. The closer you get, the happier you feel. You have the irresistible urge to immerse yourself in this light.

Everyone has unprocessed inhibiting experiences that they are aware of or that they have quickly hidden in their depth of consciousness so that they no longer have to be remembered. All of these experiences build up more or fewer blockages. These blockages have to be released to optimally enter into the liberated fulfillment of lust. Light is positive energy. These conscious and unconscious blockages dissolve in the form of shadows. It is necessary that you not only see these shadows but feel them detach from you so that you get better and better. In doing so, you free yourself from your blockages, which lead to fears, prejudices, or wrong beliefs and negatively influence, if not even prevent, your fulfillment of lust. In a short time, you will find it easier to let go of all of this. So take this path seriously.

Then you come into the light and notice how your body transforms itself into light and energy. Your body consists only of light and energy. You feel completely free. There in the light, you see your companion again, who has also become an energy body. You go to him. He takes you by the hand and leads you through a door onto a large balcony.

You see the whole universe. The stars and light nebulae, planets, and much more. It is an overwhelming sight. You feel completely free. You are now standing with your companion as a light being on the large balcony of the universe.

Your companion will lead you to the edge of the balcony. You look up at the universe and see a particularly bright light in the middle, which is approaching you. This light comes to you and envelops you completely. Now you have the deepest contact with your depth consciousness and beyond.

After you have completely cleansed your body in the ray of light, you can dissolve your physicality and become pure light and energy. You feel free. With this, you leave the material world for some time and can now dive directly into universal consciousness.

You are completely captured by this light, and it feels incredibly good. Suddenly you are at a fork in the road. The path is wide and straight. There is a sign that says "Pensionersweg." On the second path, which goes uphill, you will see a sign. It says "Path of Lust". It is interesting and you walk this path with great anticipation. You feel this joy that comes up in you and you feel very fit. You walk a little uphill and notice how good you feel with this light physical exertion. You can do it without much effort and that's a good feeling. Suddenly you arrive at a wonderful meadow. It's full of brightly colored bluebells. You hear the birds that sit in ancient, healthy trees on the edge of the meadow and chirp melodically. The butterflies are flying around you. One sits on your arm. It's a big, beautiful butterfly. It spreads its wings and flies away. You follow him with your eyes and see how he lands on a white lounger in the middle of the meadow. There it flaps its wings as if to call you. They answer the call of the butterfly full of curiosity. You slowly go to the couch. You will see a sign there. This sign says: "Liege der Lust".

You are curious and feel a pleasant tingling sensation in your stomach. You will now automatically be drawn to the lounger. You lie down on it and make yourself comfortable. Suddenly you notice how you are getting heavier and your body, completely relaxed, sinks slightly into the soft lounger. A cozy warm feeling flows through you. You feel comfortable and secure. Pleasant warmth flows into your body. You can feel it on your back, pelvis, and legs. This warmth gradually covers your whole body and you feel totally at ease.

Now she closes her eyes. You look inside yourself and you see this warmth flowing through your body like a wave. Like a warm wave from bottom to top and from top to bottom. You see this wave and realize that it is pushing a lot of dirt in front of you. This warm wave goes through your whole body, right down to the last cell of your body. It is pleasant. It washes all dirt out of your body with its warmth, all dirt is washed out. You see this wave coming up with all the dirt in front of you. Then she goes back downstairs and takes all the dirt with her. Once in your stomach, it then flows in a circle around your belly button. Very slowly it flows around in circles with all the dirt. You can see how all the dirt collects in this circle. The circle flows faster now. It is such a good feeling! The circle gets faster and faster and the faster it flows, the better you will feel. It is like a vortex that leads out of your body. You can now see all the dirt rising from your belly in a cloud of smoke. More and more smoke pours out of your stomach. The more smoke that emanates, the better you will feel. Now you don't see any dirt in the whirlpool.

You let the vortex slow down until it circles your stomach very calmly again. Not the smallest grain of dirt. Now the vortex becomes a wave again and flows through your body and you feel yourself being seized by a strong feeling of happiness. It is so wonderful to be completely free of all dirt. You can now feel the blood flowing through your body. You will feel your muscles fill up with energy. It's a very good feeling. And now you can feel the energy as it flows more and more into your penis or vagina. Your penis/vagina fills with more and more energy. You feel your strong desire. The feeling of pleasure gets stronger and stronger. It is almost unbearable. You are happy and now you feel completely free. You float freely in the room with your ever-increasing lustful feelings and give yourself to these feelings.

Then you get up. Leave the meadow and continue up the path. With every step, you feel the pleasure raging between your legs. A short time later you will see a lot of naked people in the meadow enjoying each other with relish. Suddenly they look at you and give you a friendly wave. They show that you should come to you. It is getting hotter and hotter at your step. They go to you naked and are now in the midst of these friendly, naked people. Now live out all your wild fantasies unrestrainedly. How, with whom, and as often as you want. You test everything that you are curious about and just feel like doing. Uninhibited, I just let them drift with their strong feelings of pleasure. You experience an ecstatic explosion in your depth of consciousness. That's overwhelming.

Now you will be caught by a beam of light that will carry you on again. You are still very excited and regret that you are being carried away by this wonderful place and these people. You are back at your tree of life and your companion is next to you. Still full of excitement, you look at him questioningly. He says that you are now going back into your life with all of these beautiful and strong feelings. He counts to three and you wake up joyful.

You have now programmed your deep consciousness for pleasurable feelings. It may work immediately, but you may also need to repeat it more often. Later it is enough if, before a pleasurable encounter, you let your companion in from behind from deep awareness and feel these wonderful feelings that you felt in your hypnosis. Later you don't need that either and your feelings and sensations are one with your depth consciousness. Remember the unrestrained lust that you lived out in hypnosis. That showed you the way to fulfilling and happy sex life. Let yourself be guided by it, as long as you do not harm yourself or others, anything is allowed in real life.

13.5 The bioenergetic erotic couple massage

Stress is often a pleasure killer and is always associated with emotional reactions. Our body reacts to emotional stress and forms blockages, especially in the flow of energy. This can also cause great disturbances in our sense of pleasure. I developed a bioenergetic massage for this. It releases energetic blockages in the body. Based on my experience, I can say: If these blockages are not resolved, a sustainable fight against stress and its consequences, such as fatigue, fears, psychosomatic disorders, addiction, and pleasure and potency disorders, is not possible.

That is why I have been using the bioenergetic massage that I developed and continuously improved for 20 years. And with some spectacular success. Now is the time to introduce this method to a wide audience. In my video, I am now introducing the complete full-body massage step by step in a way that is understandable and applicable for everyone for the first time. It is a video for use at home, but also for professionals who want to include this unique method in their program. It can serve as an enjoyable preventive measure or loosen existing energy blockages.

The bioenergetic massage is particularly suitable for:
stress
Loss of energy
fatigue
Psychosomatic pain
Fears
Increase in pleasure
Potency problems
Self-esteem weaknesses

Use this intensive and liberating form of massage, which, according to my comparison, has a much stronger effect than the tantric massage, also builds up an extraordinary increase in pleasurable feelings. In this relaxed, passive way, it can lead to an extremely strong orgasm, release a large number of happiness hormones and thus permanently strengthen the body and soul.

I leave out the erotic part of my video so that it can be made available to a wider audience and leave the rest to your imagination. Just let yourself go and follow your feelings. For couples, it is a wonderful way to get very close energetically. They connect more and more with each other, which is very pleasurable for the masseur and the massaged alike and creates an emotional connection over time. So it is also suitable for couples or groups who want to strengthen their feelings for each other again.

And this is how you proceed with the pleasurable massage: It is important that you, as the partner who is being massaged, are completely passive in your energies and feelings that are evoked and remain completely relaxed. You may have to learn that first. This is not about sex, but about sexual energy that you take in until it becomes so strong that you just have to discharge yourself tremendously. Do not touch your partner while doing this. The more relaxed and conscious you enjoy it, the stronger the energies and feelings become.

After you, as a masseur, have adequately energized the body according to video instructions and broken down blockages, explore the partner's erogenous zones. Build the energy there. If your partner becomes restless, calm them down with words, whispering. "Take it easy. Be completely relaxed. "Feel how your partner becomes more and more aroused. This is then a pleasure for you too. Then finally go to the genitals and continue stimulating there. Do this slowly and soulfully. When you notice that your partner is getting more and more aroused and can hardly take it anymore, whisper: "Yes, okay. You do it nicely. Be happy. "When you feel that a climax is rising, then slow down even further, causing it to explode violently. Feel this climax of your partner with.

Epilogue

Medical disclaimer

Disclaimer of liability and general information on medical topics: The content presented here is intended solely for impartial information and general further training. They do not represent a recommendation or application for the diagnostic methods, treatments, or medicinal products described or mentioned. The text does not claim to be complete, nor can the topicality, correctness, and balance of the information presented be guaranteed. The text does not in any way replace professional advice from a doctor or pharmacist and it must not be used as a basis for independent diagnosis and the start, change, or termination of treatment of illnesses. Always consult your trusted doctor if you have any health questions or complaints! As the author, I am not responsible for any inconvenience or damage that may result from using the information presented here.

14. Book Recommendation

Dr. Lutz Knoche
Video Bioenergetics massage

Stress and traumatic experiences also manifest themselves physically. Energy blockages arise.
Blockages that can weaken our body considerably.

The video shows you how you can remedy these disorders or significantly increase your general well-being. Suitable for private use or as a professional massage training.

It will be available on CD from May 2021. Duration approx. 90 minutes,

Price: € 29.95

Order and payment via PayPal

drlutzknoche@aol.com

Dr. Lutz Knoche
Luck is not a coincidence- Positive thinking is not enough

Man strives for a happy and fulfilling life. They are trying, and some are working very hard on it. But you don't seem to be quite succeeding. I got to know a lot of people. Very few were satisfied and happy, despite many positive thoughts and wishes. Why is that? In this book, you will find out which thoughts, feelings, and actions, which have so far

mostly remained undetected, keep you from fulfilling your wishes. You will learn how you can change these thoughts and feelings and thus set the course for wish fulfillment. Read how to correctly formulate your wishes so that they can be heard. Walk the path to a new level of consciousness under guidance. Read which simple method helps you to achieve your goals. You will learn step by step what you have to do to make your wishes like love, happiness, health, and success come true. Enter the existential world of your self, where body, thinking, feelings, consciousness, and universal consciousness form a unity. For the first time, an extremely effective prayer is presented in this book, with which you can achieve success even faster.
ISBN: 9783753442594

Noah Fakier und Lutz Knoche
Driven by the deep need

Stories about exciting adventures and life concepts in sexual diversity. A man confesses to his wife that he has fallen in love with another man, but that he is going to get married soon. You then embark on a path full of new erotic experiences. Three young adolescents go on their sexual journey of discovery together and experience something previously  unimaginable for them, and then everything turns out differently than they had imagined at the beginning. Two girls are deeply disappointed by the boys with whom they had their first experiences and discover how fulfilling sex can be for them in the pleasurable get-together. Two school friends collect their first sexual experiences in exciting, pleasurable games.

While one is happy and satisfied with it, the other gets to know a girl, and their friendship is put to a severe test. In their erotic stories, the authors illuminate a wide range of sexuality in an entertaining and unbiased manner.

You thus contribute to a higher process of understanding and knowledge. In Prologues, Lutz Knoche gives information on the subject of bisexuality today.

While Noah Fakier presents erotic stories about it, enriching this extraordinary book with 27 miniature drawings.

ISBN: 9783753462240

Will be published in July 2021

Noah Fakier
Drawing folder "Der Liebesreigen" for the book
Driven by the deep need

With 18 drawings

Erotic drawings about the wonderful diversity of love. The first drawing portfolio by Noah Fakier-Männer I has already attracted international attention and has become a bestseller at BoD Verlag. It can be assumed that Der Liebesreigen, with its expressive drawings, builds on this. The representation of physical love is not shown here in

pornography but in all its exciting and natural beauty. The drawings are offered in high quality on 200g paper in brilliant print and a ring binder for German collectors. A quality that pays off. Each drawing can also be separated individually. For organizational reasons, there is also a second variant, mainly for the foreign market, on 90g paper in brilliant print in bound form. Which is of course also available in Germany. You can get there by clicking on Noah Fakier you can find the best presentation on:
ISBN: 9783749498475

Pictures from the portfolio "Der Liebesreigen" - Excerpt-
Separate pictures, also for the picture frame.

18 gifts for everyone according to their taste

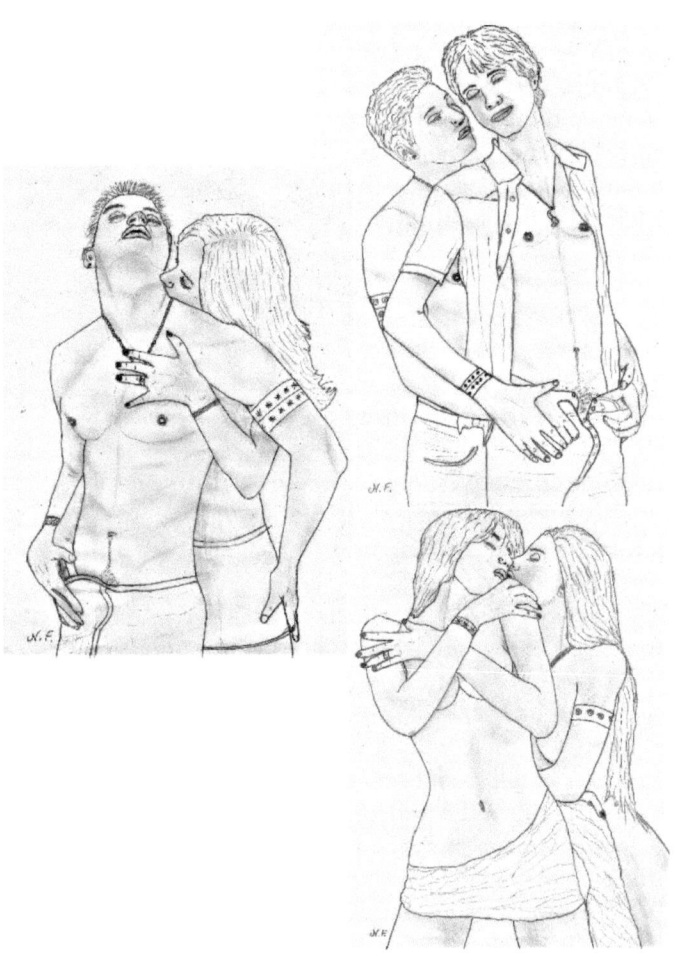

Noah Fakier
The secret stories from 1001 nights

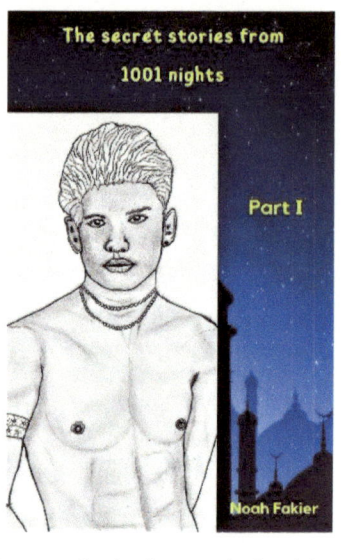

I dedicate this book to the victims who are still threatened with the death penalty for their love. The stories in this book are for all people who are free from prejudice and want to learn more about love and lust among men. There are many poems from the ancient Orient that tell about it. That was a tradition for over a thousand years. And everyone was pleased. Today all kinds of love are recognized in many countries. Only the Orient plays an inglorious role in this. In doing so, he questions his rich human history. This book ties in with the ancient traditions of the Orient. Life intolerance was a strength of the empire at that time. The true size of a country is shown in the freedom and happiness of its people who live in it. There is no substitute for money or wealth. It was like that in earlier times and it always will be. One can only hope that humanity will win again in the Orient. It's not just about abolishing the death penalty for men who love each other. It is about the freedom of all people to be able to live in love and be happy. This is a fundamental law of humanity that goes far beyond all religions in the world.

ISDN: 9783753462233

Will be published in May 2021

Drawings from:
The secret storiesfrom 1001 nights

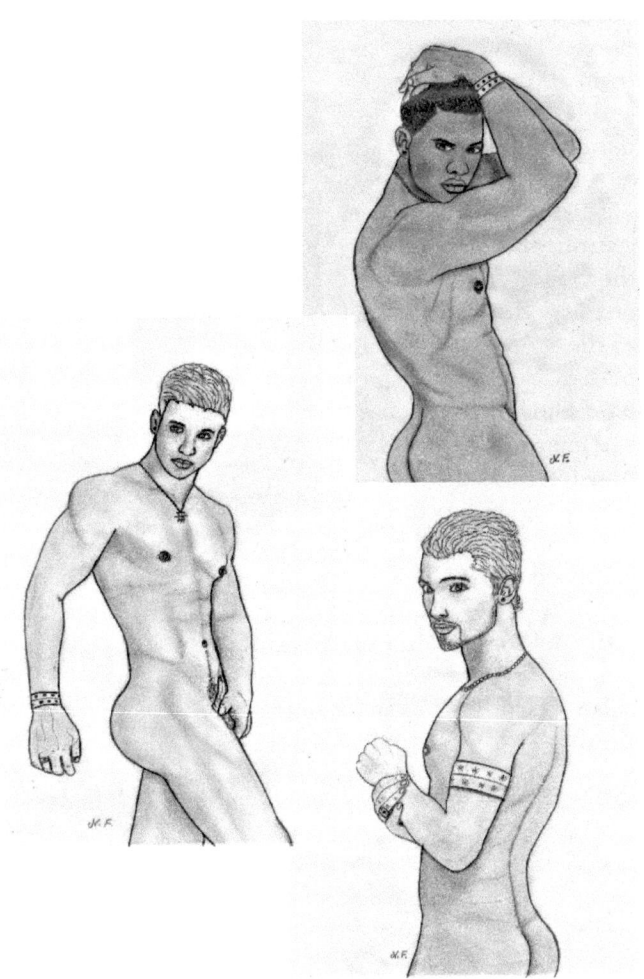

Noah Fakier
The most beautiful male drawing 2020

18 of the most beautiful erotic male nudes by Noah Fakier from his books: The secret stories from 1001 nights, Part I and II. With short quotations.

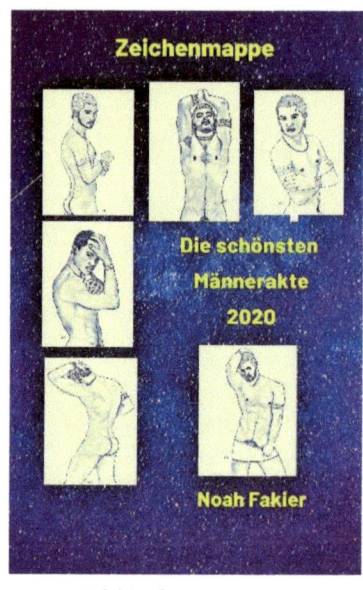

His drawings often leave a strong impression on the viewer. Noah Fakier does not draw according to the proportions that he sees, but according to his feeling of aesthetics and charisma, which is transferred to the viewer. So the pictures seem to be inspired by a very special kind. Let yourself be surprised.

DINA 4 format. In brilliant print.

Also for cutting out and framing

ISBN: 9783751906081

Drawings excerpt

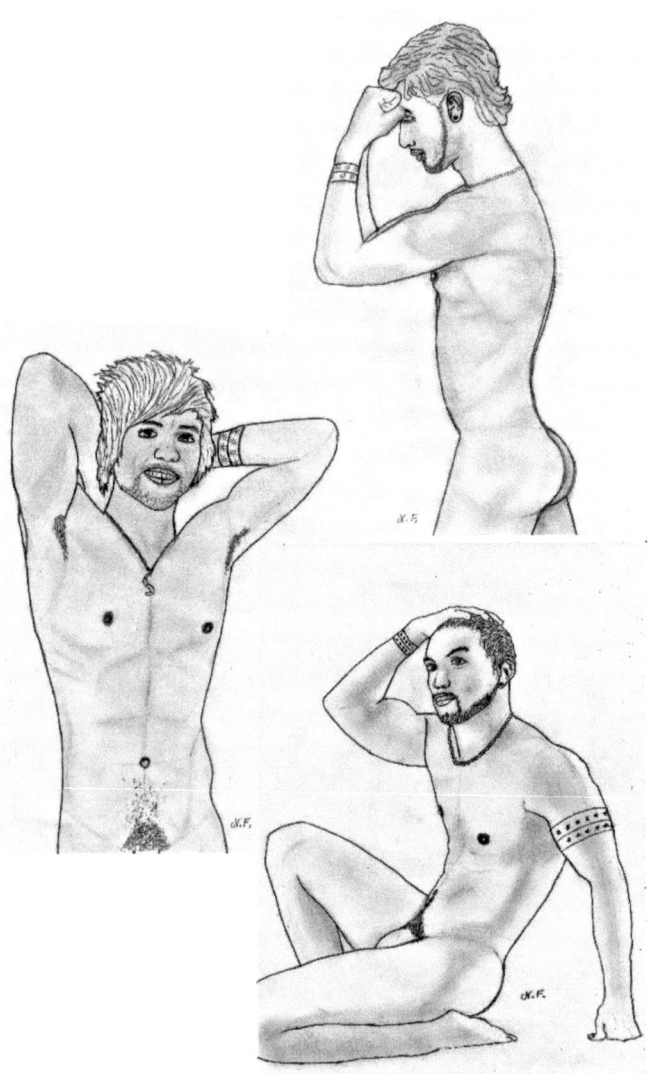